W9-BNZ-899

Po Fernando:

The Latino Family
and the
Politics of
Transformation

Un abrazo,

David T. Abalos

The Latino Family
and the
Politics of
Transformation

David T. Abalos

Praeger Series in Transformational Politics
and Political Science
Theodore L. Becker, *Series Adviser*

Westport, Connecticut
London

Library of Congress Cataloging-in-Publication Data

Abalos, David T.
    The Latino family and the politics of transformation / David T.
Abalos.
        p.   cm. (Praeger series in transformational
    politics and political science, ISSN 1061–5261)
    Includes bibliographical references and index.
    ISBN 0–275–94527–8 (alk. paper)
    ISBN 0–275–94809–9 (pbk.)
    1. Hispanic American families. I. Title.
    E184.S75A62   1994
    306.85'08968—dc20   93–19612

British Library Cataloguing in Publication Data is available.

Copyright © 1993 by David T. Abalos

All rights reserved. No portion of this book may be
reproduced, by any process or technique, without the
express written consent of the publisher.

Library of Congress Catalog Card Number: 93–19612
ISBN: 0–275–94527–8
      0–275–94809–9 (pbk.)
ISSN: 1061–5261

First published in 1993

Praeger Publishers, 88 Post Road West, Westport, CT 06881
An imprint of Greenwood Publishing Group, Inc.

Printed in the United States of America

The paper used in this book complies with the
Permanent Paper Standard issued by the National
Information Standards Organization (Z39.48–1984).

10 9 8 7 6 5 4 3

For Celia Dorantes Abalos and Veronica M. Abalos
Celia Hernandez Dorantes, Vicki Abalos Goodall,
and Angie Abalos Gomez

IN MEMORIAM

Luz Gil Avalos
Luis José Avalos
Maria Hernandez Hernandez
Marge Abalos Corbin
Salvador J. Abalos

Contents

Acknowledgments

This book is especially dedicated to my wife and my daughter, my sisters, my mother, my mother-in-law, and my grandmothers—four generations of Mejicanas/Latinas who have experienced, and continue to do so, the wounds of patriarchy. Not in spite of, but because of this archetypal challenge, these women and all Latina women have earned the right to refuse to continue to collaborate with those aspects of their inherited culture and with men who prolong this deadly story that legitimizes male domination.

Through writing this book I have come to rediscover aspects of my past as a Latino male, husband, and father that I had to reject and then reclaim and redeem. But, also, I came to realize that it was necessary for me to begin the creation of a new story for myself and my community regarding Latino male and Latina female relationships in the service of transformation.

To the Latino males of my generation, especially my brothers, Sal and Louis, and for David Jerome and Matthew, my two sons, who represent the third generation of Mejicano males in my family in this country, it will be our challenge to name, confront, and reject the inherited archetypal stories and ultimate ways of knowing and living that have crippled our relationships to our selves and to women, so that we can create more loving and just relationships.

I especially thank Celia, my wife, and Veronica, my daughter, for refusing to become matriarchal, a rebellious spinoff from the drama of patriarchy. Instead they have sought to establish their own places as full persons with masculine and feminine wholeness.

Teresita Fernandez-Viña taught me so much about the deep love and courage being demonstrated by Latinas as single parents who struggle daily to preserve the family. She not only cares for her own child, Elizabeth, but has become an advocate for all children and families. My friend and colleague, Emily Jane Style, co-director of the National S.E.E.D. Program, has read and critiqued many of my papers. I am deeply grateful for her support and encouragement over the years. I thank with a warm embrace Patricia Hunt Perry, who stepped in at a crucial point to assist me in finishing this book. My colleagues and friends at Seton Hall University were a continuous source of emotional and intellectual support, especially my dear Latino brother Frank Morales and the marvelous staff of the Puerto Rican Institute: Dr. Lillian Perez, Lucia Kassela, and Maribel Marsden. Ann Rebhan has for many years been an outstanding example of a woman and mother who raised her children with great courage and love while she provided excellent care for others as a deeply compassionate nurse in our health services. I very much appreciate the support that I received throughout the writing of this book from Gerry Pire, Dean Jerry Hirsch, and Provost Bernhard Scholz.

My students were invaluable in helping me to sort out the mysteries of the Latino family. I am grateful to Cenci Hernandez-Cancio, Myrna Santiago, Cesar Gallegos, Anna Cabrera, Patricia Garcia, Jeff Avila, Ivette Santiago, Miriam Lopez, Juan Chavez, and Sheila Marmon.

There is developing in the Latino community a new generation of Latina and Latino scholars and administrators from whom I have drawn much intellectual and personal strength. They are administering, teaching, writing, studying, living, and telling our stories with great commitment and brilliance. Among these are Alberto Pulido, Maxine Lisboa, David Carrasco, Angel Millan, Luis Salgado, Maria Vizcarrondo, Lara Medina, Gilbert Cadena, Joan Bloustein, Edwin Hernandez, Lourdes Soto, and Jose Adames.

The theory of transformation has been for me both a guide and a grounding for all of my teaching, writing, and scholarship. I could not have contributed what I have to the knowledge of our Latino community without the help and guidance of my friend and colleague Manfred Halpern, who rediscovered and retold for our time the theory of transformation. It was he who, often under very difficult circumstances, brilliantly kept alive for me and for many others the light and wisdom of the countertradition of transformation.

I also want to warmly thank Joe Holland. He cajoled, encouraged, and, finally, convinced me to write this book—reading, editing, and critiquing the chapters. Without his sense of urgency that a book on the Latino family was needed, I doubt that I would have chosen to take on such an endeavor.

Finally, I would like to thank my editors, Professor Ted Becker and Dan Eades, for their encouragement, editing, and genuine friendship throughout the writing of the manuscript.

Introduction

The Latino family, as well as the family in general, is in deep trouble in our society. After much searching and pain the reality is that there is no such thing as an ideal family. Nevertheless, an ideal model has been embraced for centuries by the Latino culture, one similar to that of the fundamentalist movement in the United States: a patriarchal family where the mother performs the usual gender tasks of the household, the children are all reared to have respect for authority, and they are all God-fearing. Trying to live such an ideal type is not easy, has contradictions, and eventually becomes dysfunctional. For example, Presidents Reagan and Bush, who romanticized this view of the family, also supported economic policies that forced women into the workplace in order to make it possible for the family to survive.

Other idealized images of the family continue to lull us to sleep. We are shown in the media the lovely wives and children of politicians and business leaders. What we are seeing is merely external appearances and not what actual qualities of relationships are necessary to hold members of a family together.

Recent demographic studies have exposed the illusions of the model held up for us to emulate. Divorce is increasing; teenage pregnancy is growing throughout the nation; stepfamilies are commonplace; test-tube babies are removing the father altogether; frozen sperm are contested as property in divorce proceedings; single or divorced mothers as parents are the norm in many urban areas; and more couples are living together without any promise of commitment. Thus, the idealized nuclear family consisting of two parents, two or three children, the dog, and the house in the suburbs is already an anachronism.

Alternative family structures are being created. More women are consciously choosing to have children and not to marry; gay people are celebrating marriage ceremonies and adopting children; divorced gays are setting up families with their children and lovers; grandparents (often a grandmother) are rearing grandchildren; a brother and sister are raising each other; a homeless child is being cared for by an adult. Thus we have today in our society many kinds of families living side by side. The language of deviance, ideal types, legitimacy, and stability is not very useful. We live in a time where every sixteen seconds there is an act of child or spouse abuse in this country. The greatest violence in our society takes place in the bedrooms of our nation.

Furthermore, what is at stake here is not the nuclear nor even the extended family but the future quality of the relationships that link members of the family together. In order to go beyond external and superficial appearances, we need a theory that allows us to see in a new way and to ask fundamentally new kinds of questions. We have to ask what actual relationships are being practiced in a particular family relative to a particular problem and what specific drama is being enacted.

In this book we will be reenvisioning the family from the perspective of a theory of transformation that will be fully explained in the chapters ahead, but especially in Chapter One. In this chapter we will fully explore a theory of transformation that allows us to relate theory to the reality of daily life. We will apply the theory of transformation to the Latino family and provide many examples taken from everyday life so that we will be able to see the Latino family in motion and, perhaps more important, understand the underlying causes of its dilemma. Thus, if we can get "behind the scenes," so to speak, and analyze the family from an archetypal perspective, we will be able to go beyond the usual stereotypes that were never real. Then we will be free to transform it for the better.

Archetypal analysis does not allow us to stereotype either negatively or positively. What counts is to be able to see what the theory presented here will allow us to do: name the relationships present, the relationships that are forbidden, the patterns that are breaking, the alternative linkages being created, the archetypal dramas or stories involved, and in the service of what way of life—emanation, incoherence, deformation, or transformation—we are living the life of the family.

This represents the steps and language of archetypal analysis that will be fully explained in the first chapter and applied to the Latino family throughout the book. For example, when we ask if the family is made up of a mother and father and three children or of a grandmother and her grandson, or what their levels of education and income are, we really know very little. What provides us with a deeper insight is knowing the story or the drama that the family members are living. For example, suppose it is revealed through the story of the father that he was abused as a child but never dealt with the hurt and anger. As a result he enters into a marriage carrying the scars of deformation that have not healed but have been repressed. In rearing his own children, he may tell himself, and it may look to his wife and to those around them, that he is strict and "spanks" his children to correct them. In fact what he may be doing is repeating the archetypal drama that he thought he rejected in his own father and mother.

As we will see in this kind of analysis, it is not ever enough to consciously reject or leave our actual parents behind. We are also required to enter into the deeper realms of our lives in order to empty ourselves not only of our concrete parents but also of the archetype or underlying forming sources that gave our parents their mysterious power over us—that is, the archetype of the mother and father that are the grounding sources of our continuing behavior. Thus the wife, on her part, may suspect that something is wrong but she has been shaped by a drama of uncritical obedience to authority and therefore yields her right to question, because her husband is exercising the authority legitimized by her father. Both father and husband inherited sacred dramas that gave them permission to dominate women. If a woman—on this deeper level—is dominated by the archetype of the father, she is unable to confront her husband because she too is entangled in the archetype of the father. The archetype, since it is projected onto the husband, means that, for all intents and purposes, her husband becomes her father.

The children, as they grow older, may also sense the ambivalence in the father who only knows how to show love by punishing. This may lead them to forms of rebellion and hatred so they shout that they will never be like their father. But because they see only the external manifestations of the drama of an abusive father, and are not conscious of the underlying powerful source of the archetype of the father, they will in their own adult parenting repeat the same drama of the abusive father.

Children can intuit, if not articulate, many problems in the relationship between their parents. The most obvious problem to children are parents who talk constantly about love but never exchange any affection or tenderness. The unresolved and repressed anger suffered by the father as a child breeds other kinds of deformation. Deformation is the creation of the fundamentally new, which is also fundamentally worse. Deformation is anything that diminishes our humanity. Thus to get revenge on their parents, children turn to drugs or liquor, get pregnant, go crazy intentionally, do poorly in school, or, perhaps what is even worse, repress their anger so that they walk around like live bombs that will explode sooner or later in irrational and terrible ways. In Chapter Two, we will demonstrate how the home is a microcosm of the wider society and how various archetypal dramas and stories (patriarchy, matriarchy, possessive love, the battered wife) are practiced within the context of the family. Then we will show how these stories either prepare or disable Latino youth for a particular kind of politics.[1]

Nothing is a purely personal, private problem. Our dramas always have four faces—personal, political, historical, and sacred—which will be explained in the context of this book. But why do I speak of the sacred here? As stated earlier, we are all in the grip of living, archetypal forces that emerge from the depths; this is the realm of the sacred. The sacred is a mystery that shapes all of our lives decisively. Therefore, my supposedly private problems affect the way I shape relationships in my domestic environment and, therefore determine the politics of what we can and need to do as a family. In addition, if we are blindly repeating history without being conscious of it, we are robbed of our ability to break with

the past and put new and better relationships (that is, alternative
dramas) in place, thereby creating a new beginning, a new history,
a new politics. Finally, because these are sacred and powerful dramas that decisively shape our lives, all the rationalizing in the world
will not cast out these sacred dramas until we consciously choose
an alternative lord, one that assists us in the creation of more loving
and just relationships.

What if Latino parents are lamed by archetypal dramas that they
have never recognized or acknowledged? Some parents have indeed
intuited and practiced their stories in the service of transformation.
But too many are caught by the inherited dysfunctional dramas of
our culture and feel there is nothing that can be done. However,
the theory of transformation described herein can empower Latinos
to recognize the destructive dramas in which they are enmeshed.
This new realization can make creative choices possible for all. The
theory of transformation is based on the understanding that people
can change and can realize they have choices. So a person who has
been acting out a dysfunctional inherited archetypal drama can
come to see that drama in all of its terror, reject it, and choose
another way of living and being a parent. Consequently, Chapter
Three will trace the inherited archetypal dramas of patriarchy and
matriarchy across several generations in a Latino family. We will
see how and why patriarchy has deeply wounded the Latino family.
The emergence of the matriarchy was a very important choice made
as a response to the collapse of the patriarchal drama. But, in its
own turn, matriarchy will also have to yield to new archetypal
responses created by the current crisis of Latino families.

What makes change for the better so difficult for the Latino family
is the external reality of the public realm in U.S. society, which is
itself permeated by the archetypal dramas of power and deformation. Thus, Latinos and most people of color are often severely
hindered in their attempt to create alternative families. They are
being systematically deprived by structural violence from having a
loving and nurturing family life. The poor are almost always blamed
for their poverty. Cutbacks in funds for dependent children, prenatal care, day care services, Head Start, food stamps, rent allow-
ances, health care for children, and other such programs take on a
vindictive character. The predominating archetypal way of life of
the body politic of the United States is the way of life of incoherence.

This is a way of life that legitimizes the pursuit of power, status, and prestige. Threats to the powerful are often resisted by resorting to forms of exclusion and violence. For example, a politician who needs the European-American, white vote might shift necessary funds away from essential services to poor people and into military budgets. This tactic to preserve power makes life fundamentally worse for others. Such a politician practices deformation. Some politicians tell the poor or communities of color that such policies are for their own good, that they must learn to fend for themselves rather than go on welfare. In reality the policies are a form of greed and fear that is intended to keep already impoverished citizens and children dependent and even incapacitated. Acts of deformation on the personal will, on the family level, or in the public realm are the same archetypal way of destructive death. The politician as a kind of abusive father does not want his children to become mature, critical citizens.

Chapter Four will be especially concerned with dramas in the service of incoherence and deformation that are so prevalent within Latino (and all other) families owing to assaults by the more powerful sectors of the society. As long as Latinos and others persist in living the drama of the patriarchal family, a wounding of all the members of the family will continue. The violence within the family and the external assault has put Latino families in great danger. As Latina women move to change their lives they are often threatened by physical and, equally damaging, psychological violence from Latino males who cannot relate to Latinas as equals. But there is a deeper issue. Intellectually, many Latino males may say they wish to live a mutual life with women, but the underlying archetypal dramas of possessive love and patriarchy have not been rooted out from their souls. Latina women, for their part, must refuse to perpetuate the stories of the martyr/victim and insist on a full partnership with men. As a matter of fact, the greatest service that can be performed for the society at large is to rear children in the service of transformation—that is, in families that love them, nourish them, and prepare them for compassionate living with others.

However, one cannot be naive about the larger society. Somewhere the cycle of deformation must be broken so that the next generation is not lost. I, as a Mejicano/Chicano, cannot forget that prior to 1940 only 1 percent of all Chicano children in the Southwest were in school. Somebody had made a conscious, political decision that Mejicanos did not need schooling because their future was as stoop labor in the fields. This was institutionalized deformation that crippled a whole generation of young Chicanos so they could not be prepared to do anything with their lives.

Recently there has been much discussion about how it is necessary for U.S. society to educate and generally take care of the next generation of children of color because it is, to put it bluntly, in America's own best economic interests in an era of global competition. But this is a rational solution for an underlying archetypal story. The powerful are still obsessed by the fear of giving too much, of redistributing power. To save the system that has been constructed for their benefit seems the logical thing for them to do. But the real issues are matters having to do with inherited archetypal dramas of power, privilege, superiority, racism, and classism. These archetypes are concrete manifestations of the deep sources of destructive exclusion in the service of deformation. If they are not confronted, there will be no solution.

Thus, there is plenty of work for all of us. Latinos and people of color must decide to stop participating in the crippling of their own children. Politically, we have to go beyond our own homes to confront the larger polity with its lack of social concern, a lack that can no longer be tolerated. People of color are changing the face of America. In fact, communities of color, taken together, will soon be the majority: thus for U.S. society to exclude them is to mortally wound its own future. We cannot give up: power corrupts and absolute power corrupts absolutely; but, conversely, powerlessness corrupts and absolute powerlessness corrupts all of us absolutely.

It is necessary for us not only to expose the problem but to create alternatives that are more just and compassionate. In this regard I have learned much from my students from all cultural backgrounds. For the past fifteen years I have taught a course on Strategies of Transformation in which I invite students to write about their families. Almost without exception, the students eagerly seek to analyze their families. Through the discipline of the theory of transformation they speak of the various archetypal relationships, dramas, and ways of life and deformation they have experienced. What I have learned from reading their papers is that regardless of gender, racial, ethnic, or socioeconomic background, the majority of the students walk into class having experienced one or several of the following traumas: alcohol abuse, drug abuse, physical abuse, sexual abuse, or the trauma of separation due to death or divorce. I regard these traumas as symptoms of deeper, underlying, and unresolved archetypal dramas that are unconsciously taking their toll.

One paper I especially remember was written by a European-American woman from a wealthy family who was unaware of archetypal dramas. However, in writing her paper, she discovered some alarming patterns. Her grandparents drank heavily, all day long. Then she realized that her parents were doing the same thing. For the first time she admitted that she too was involved in the same drama. It was painful for her to admit that they were all alcoholics. In another paper, a young woman, also from a European-American background, revealed that her drinking was related to fear of affection. Whenever she sought affection she drank heavily. Earlier she had come to the conclusion that she was an alcoholic. However, in the middle of her paper, she revolted against this facile conclusion. The liquor was a buffer to hide a deeper drama, a deformational experience of sexual abuse by a family member. To hide this painful, deeper archetypal drama of abuse that made her ashamed of sex, she had to numb herself before she could accept any affection. The discovery in both of these life histories of deep archetypal dramas that had been controlling their lives was an enormous help to these young women. Both students wrote of their willingness to begin a new life by consciously breaking these archetypal dramas and choosing an alternative that would liberate them to grow and to free them from continuing to enact their lives in the service of deformation.

Thus writing these papers is a political, personal, historical, and sacred act that empowers the student to name their oppression, reject it, and choose alternative ways of relating and acting out dramas in the service of transformation. The students, in telling the stories of their lives, are really describing archetypal dramas and ways of life and deformation. To be able to point them out and analyze them is to guide them to the possibility of altering their lives at the core of their very being. In writing such papers, students are able to move from the affective to the intellectual, from the personal to the political, historical, and sacred aspects of their lives. The family is their crucible. They now realize that they have the opportunity to end destructive relationships and dramas so that they can, in the words of the alchemists, dissolve base metals and recoagulate the elements in such a way that the gold of the inner self is discovered.

These papers helped me test the theory of transformation, made me more aware of how all of us, from whatever cultural backgrounds, need to be aware of our archetypal inheritance. We need to provide credible examples of how to empty ourselves of the destructive inherited stories of our lives and how to learn to enact fundamentally more loving and just relationships—that is, to practice the politics of transformation in the family. Too often the students blamed individual family members, their culture, themselves, or God for their families' shortcomings. It was like beating the air because too often they could not name the patterns or search out the origins of the relational patterns that caused so much pain.

Latina and Latino students and students of color, because they were usually from backgrounds of economic poverty, often identified many of their familial problems with poverty and/or racism. There is much truth in this, but middle-class students of color, in most cases, had the same problems. The saddest papers were those in which students expressed a self-hatred and hatred or dislike of their culture. Thus some would seek to blame the culture as defective and themselves as victims. The solution they sought was to identify with Anglo-Saxon familial patterns that provided autonomy to all and none of that possessive Latino "stuff."

Some Latinos and Latinas realized that the answer was not to go back and romanticize the inherited archetypal patterns, dramas, and ways of life. They also concluded that the answer was not to assimilate into the European-American family patterns, nor to turn to violence to hold together the crumbling family. The realization came that something more imaginative and risky had to be attempted: to create one's own family, to grow one's own family and culture in the service of transformation. This latter choice involved breaking with those archetypal patterns both inherited from the past and imposed by the dominant culture.

Transformation is meant to painfully, but lovingly, and redemptively reacquire the best of the Latino inheritance and to reject that which is destructive. Therefore, Chapter Five will look at two examples of the struggle to transform the Latino family: the story of

Lucia and Tomas, two characters in the excellent revolutionary film
Lucia, directed by Humberto Solas, and the true story of a Latino
couple, Luis and Carmen. The archetypal analysis of this film and
the stories of these marriages and families gives us an insight into
the pervasiveness and the cost of patriarchy in the Latino family
and culture. All Latinos have to pay the price, to empty their souls
of inherited archetypal dramas, and to create new dramas that allow
them to live more human lives. Latinos badly need stories of transformation that show ordinary people struggling to transform their
personal, political, historical, and sacred lives.

Perhaps often without their knowing it, this is the true heritage
that our mothers and fathers bequeathed to us. Together they took
the decision, even though events may have thrust it upon them, to
leave their homelands, to journey to another country, and to build
and nourish a new life. This is precisely what transformation demands of all of us—that we uproot the old, embark on a journey,
and, when we arrive there, to plant and nourish the new *milpas*,
fields of maize, which in the ancient Mayan tradition was the food
of the gods, intended to raise up new generations of the sacred.
Each generation will follow the same divine/agricultural/mother
earth rhythm—to root out the drought of deformation and to put
down new seeds that are nourished and watered as the new harvest.
To raise a family is indeed sacred work. It will be my task in this
book to discern between the sacred sources that inspire us and to
choose from among the underlying sources only those that invite
us to fulfill the core drama of transformation and to participate as
cocreators in building more loving and compassionate families.

Finally, I could not write the book about the Latino family without reflecting and doing archetypal analysis in a very personal way,
a way that permits a vision of many aspects of Latino families in
motion. For several years, I have spoken about these dramas to
many people, both Latino and non-Latinos, and have found the
response to be both encouraging and provocative. What I have come
to learn is that it is not only the Latino family but *all* American
families that are either not aware of or are rejecting transformation.
Another way of saying this is that Latino culture as a whole is not
the problem; there are stories, not only within the Latino culture
but also in the larger society, that do not allow the self and the
community to participate in creating new and better relationships

and dramas in the service of transformation and that, as a result, ultimately wound its members.

To further test the validity of archetypal analysis, I have shared these ideas with members of my family. Thinking through and feeling these dramas and their powerful presence deeply affected us. There is no escaping this painful, personal dimension because without it this book, as so many others, would simply become another volume based on abstractions. Furthermore, the telling of our Latino story is a political, historical, sacred, as well as a personal challenge, because it affirms that none of us is alone and that the heart of politics is what we can and need to do *together*, that we all repeat or create new turning points in our histories and that the sacred, either negatively or for good, continues to create through us. I deeply thank the spirit for coming in this way so that family can become for Latinos and all others a merciful and loving haven that prepares us to participate in the continuous creation of the world with justice and compassion.

NOTE

1. Throughout this book, the term "Latinos" encompasses *both* males (Latinos) and females (Latinas). When either gender is referred to specifically, the terms "Latina," "Latinas," or "Latina women" and "Latino" or "Latino males" will be used

The Latino Family
and the
Politics of
Transformation

Chapter One

A Theory of Transformation

In all my borned days I never seed
Nothing unto like this here a-fore!
'Course I ain't really been lookin'
For nothin' like this either.

"Pogo," 1955

A theory of transformation will serve as our grounding, our guide, as we reenvision, reinterpret, and reclaim the Latino family. Ours is a theory that empowers us to participate in the core drama of transformation—together with our neighbor and our sacred sources. This participation allows us to choose between ways of life and death and to bring together the personal, political, historical, and sacred faces of our personal and familial lives. By applying theory to practice we will be able to see the Latino family in motion as its members struggle to re-create the family in the service of transformation.

To understand, live, and practice transformation, we need a theory that will help us go beyond the dire descriptions of what is. The present theoretical talk of structures and functions, periods of equilibrium, and the maintenance of systems is of little use in helping to build a new and more fruitful, nourishing way of life.

None of us has ever seen a political structure or system sit down and have a hamburger or walk across a busy street. But we have all seen families enact concrete relationships and stories that become systemic or routinized ways of doing things—that is, as human beings we act out inherited patterns or, as most often happens, we unconsciously allow inherited patterns and stories to shape our human behavior. People become a part of the abstract system by allowing themselves to be made into robotic extensions who carry out programmed behavior.

A NEW THEORETICAL PERSPECTIVE

The very word "theory" can be intimidating because for many, theory is taught as a set of abstract principles that are difficult to understand or put into everyday language and practice. Economic, sociological, or political theory, as a study of abstract principles and relationships, can be very alienating. However, in this book, theory will be reinterpreted, re-visioned, and, it is hoped, re-experienced in very personal terms and applied in a concrete way.

The theory that will be described and applied in this book was developed by Manfred Halpern.[1] It is an extraordinary theory in its ability to grasp the intimate connection between individual human behavior, politics, history, and the underlying deeper meaning of our lives. Furthermore, this theory gives us an opportunity to understand and participate in the core drama of transformation wherein we choose between four ultimate ways of life—one of which ends in destructive death. The reader will be provided with an analysis of these four ultimate choices and given the opportunity to participate in constructing new and personal manifestations of more just and loving archetypal dramas and relationships. To understand what is meant by archetypal ways of life, dramas, and relationships is to know something crucial about how life hangs together.

In addition, this theory will provide a way of recognizing the simultaneous unity of the four faces of our being: personal, political, historical, and sacred. In addition, it will enable us to understand and analyze the archetypal stories or dramas of our lives that particularly affect the Latino family, such as the stories of patriarchy, possessive love, and matriarchy. Finally, it will present a means of critiquing and changing the reality of our lives.

This theory, as all good theories should, provides us with an interrelated set of testable generalizations, which fulfill the following requirement. It allows us to deal with problems that are central to all human relations, formulated in terms and concepts that are not culture-bound. Such a theory also must allow us to use the same concepts and interrelated hypotheses for intrapersonal, interpersonal, and intergroup relations.

I propose to provide the outlines of Halpern's theory here and to use it in the struggle to analyze and develop a politics of transformation for *la familia Latina* in the United States. This theory should help us understand how the relationships connecting Latinas and Latinos in the family are being used creatively or destructively. The theory can enable us to see that the only viable alternative to an uncritical loyalty to the inherited forms of the Latino family, (i.e., to a way of life that dedicates the members of the family to the pursuit of self-interest, or to violence, one that results in personal, familial, and political dysfunction) is transformation, a way of life committed to the creation of fundamentally new and better relationships.

What is at stake here is our willing and creative participation in the story of transformation. This story arises out of our experiences of transformation. Once we have experienced transformation we do not believe in it—that is, we do not turn it into a dogma. Instead we must risk our faith, meaning that we must experience transformation again and again. Transformational theory is above all participation in the drama of the life, death, and resurrection of sacred sources in the stories of our lives. Therefore, it is not a question of proving the theory, or convincing someone, and certainly not demonstrating it to someone else. What is so compelling and truthful regarding this theory is that people can live it and test it with their own experience. Transformation helps us make sense of our own lives and see how the whole of our experiences hang together. Let us begin to provide our theoretical and conceptual framework by retelling and reenvisioning the story of creation and the journey of transformation.

RETELLING THE STORY OF THE CREATION OF
THE COSMOS: THE CORE DRAMA OF
TRANSFORMATION

Ein-sof, the name given to the god beyond god in the ancient Jewish mystical tradition, created first of all the core drama of life: the archetypal drama of transformation, a three-act drama that must be enacted again and again. Why? Because the source of all sacred sources is still in the process of continuous creation.[2] From the beginning, creation was intended to bring forth the fundamentally new and better. The core drama of transformation requires participation in all of its three acts between the deepest source and us, the concretely created. *Ein-sof* is not perfect (i.e., finished): why else endless creation? Neither our sacred source nor we are perfect. So together with *ein-sof* we disconnect again and again in order to reemerge in a new and better unity. But our participation demands our freedom to say yes or no. Who are the participants? We humans are, since we are the only creation able to persist in transformation without a preprogrammed outcome.

Other key participants are archetypal, sacred forces or gods. Why gods, plural? Because we could not feel deeply attracted to act I, the service of the way of life of emanation, and be inspired to remain in it and to arrest and consolidate it unless an archetypal, sacred force or god was also free to say no and to separate itself from the core drama and hold us there. Similarly, we could not say no to act I but agree to remain arrested in act II, unless an archetypal source, the god of incoherence, could separate itself from the core drama and hold us there. We could not be sucked into the abyss of deformation unless an archetypal force, symbolized by Satan, had the power to pull us down as we give into fantasies of gender, nation, race, or religion to cover our insecurity.

Why do we need these other gods, or archetypal forces, that can frustrate the core drama created by *ein-sof*? This is not a puppet play. The drama of transformation has to offer us and the archetypal forces the capacity and freedom to say no and yes to the core drama. Therefore, the lord of emanation can choose to arrest the drama in act I, and we can be overwhelmed and continue to repress the new insights in order to allow act I to remain a viable container. We cannot act at all without archetypal sources to pattern our actions; but neither are archetypal forces complete without us. For this reason we have to ask always which god, or archetypal source, inspires us.

Why is there evil? All archetypal forces in the core drama of transformation are free to act once they have been created by the deepest source of our being. These sacred, archetypal sources repress their knowledge of the deepest ground of our being so that we cannot have any access to the god beyond god nor can *ein-sof* reach us through our link to them. Evil comes into the world when we and the archetypal force symbolized as Satan betray the drama of transformation and move into consciously created destructive death or deformation.

Ein-sof began creation by creating the core drama of transformation because only that drama fulfills the need for persistent transformation. But the source of all sources gave us and the archetypal sources the freedom to prevent or to participate in fragmentation and destruction. Still evil is not a necessary by-product of freedom or transformation. We can choose to move through the core drama together with *ein-sof* again and again without exiting from the drama and descending into the abyss of destruction; a course of action that makes life fundamentally new but worse. To so choose is to continuously say no to the archetypal lords who enchant us in emanation, enchain us in fragments of power, or suck us into the abyss. We have to free ourselves from these sacred sources, to be filled anew by our deepest sacred source. *Ein-sof* does not stand by passively but enters the drama again and again. But the god beyond god cannot command transformation; therefore the ground of our being needs our participation to renew and widen transformation.

In this drama all of us can practically participate in terms of the structure of the core drama of transformation. Increasingly in the modern age the most important choice is between deformation and transformation. To choose life together is to participate with each other, and to choose the god of transformation to lead us is to be renewed by *ein-sof*.[3]

There is a marvelously redemptive aspect to the core drama of transformation, which consists of our ability to realize in what drama we were caught and in what way of life we enacted a decision. We are now free to reject the destructive dramas and ways of life and to choose more just and loving relationships in the service of transformation. This participatory nature of the core drama prevents us from losing precious time by punishing ourselves because of hurt pride, guilt, or anger. We are now empowered to cancel our guilt by creating alternatives in such a way that we simultaneously accept responsibility for what was done and decide to do something to heal the injury that was caused by living destructive dramas.

This great blessing of the core drama flows from the inherent mercy of the source of sources. It is a witness to the inherent dynamic of the universe, one based on love. It is never too late either for ourselves or for others. For this reason we must not freeze ourselves or others in stereotypes because stasis violates the very nature of the universe, which is a constant invitation to cocreate the universe.

Our four principal gods were there from the beginning of the creation. The god of emanation demands orthodox truth and omnipotence and did not want ein-sof—or Tao, or God, or the Cloud of Unknowing, or Allah, or Ometeotl—to create human beings because human beings would be both sacred and concrete beings. As such they would have a necessary role in creation. Human beings are necessary because the source of all sources, the undifferentiated source, who has no concreteness, needed human beings to give creation a concrete face. This necessary cocreation between the source of sources and human beings made us objects of jealousy to the god of a final and fixed truth, since this god of emanation could only dominate the realm of a once-for-all creation. We are both sacred and concrete. We have two faces: through us the deepest source has real feet and through us can continue to create. But cocreation can take place only if we realize our inner sacredness by embarking on the journey of transformation.[4]

THE THREE ACTS OF THE CORE DRAMA OF TRANSFORMATION

This journey has three acts (see Figure 1).[5] The gods of emanation, or orthodox truth, do not want us to break the container in act I, scene 1. They assault us with feelings of sin, shame, and guilt and raise up priests to sermonize us and the state authorities to enforce

Figure 1
The Core Drama of Transformation

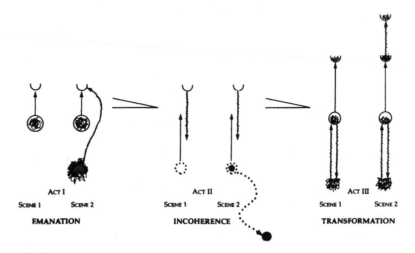

obedience. The resulting stability keeps the priests and warriors in power. The few control the many in large part because this god of jealousy possesses the people; the people, on their part, obey because they are given security. This is the sacred origin of repression. Repression means that people unconsciously control themselves. All resistance is surrendered because they come to love the master, to love the god who tricks them into participating in their own subjugation. In this manner the journey is made heretical. People are reluctant to depart; they are arrested in their flowing forth from *ein-sof*.

This stasis clearly impoverishes all of us. The emphasis is on continuity and cooperation with the status quo. We are forbidden to create conflict or change; our justice is security, the cost is the sacredness within our selfhood. In addition, cut off from our deepest sources, caught in the embrace of this orthodox god, we cannot develop a new consciousness, new linkages to others, or shared goals. We are stillborn. This is the god of the sociologists of religion, who study this god of institutionalized religion without knowing it; as a result only symptoms are studied because sociologists do not know the realm of underlying sacred sources. Therefore, they can only marvel at the power of a reified religion that possesses its citizens to perform functions for a society. This is the god that Marx and Freud rejected, but in the process they, like the sociologists, rejected the sacred. Our story will allow us to reject this god who seeks to be "the" god and to identify and choose between our other three major gods.[6]

The whole thrust of the cosmos is to be in permanent creation, which means to enact the core drama again and again. We can realize transformation only in regard to one aspect of our life at a time; transformation is never total. The men and women of the countertradition, which is at least 2,600 years old, held the following in common: they recognized the rise of deep incoherence in their society; to get out of incoherence, they realized that they had to end previous forms of emanation; as they looked for alternative ways to shape life, they discovered archetypes—that is, the underlying patterning forces of which all concrete relationships and all concrete dramas in which we live our lives are manifestations; they came to see the cosmos as one of continuous creation and therefore saw transformation as our personal participation in that process; they then saw the connection between our personal, political, historical, and sacred faces as essential to participating in continuous creation; all were radical because they sought to go to the root of the issues by searching for the ultimate source of the fundamentally new and better.

Some of those who explored the theory and practice of transformation were Heraclitus (6th century B.C.), Lao-Tse (6th century B.C.), Buddha (died 483 B.C.), Plato (died 347 B.C.), Jesus, Moses Maimonides (died 1204), al-Farabi (died 950), Ibn Arabi (1165–1240), Meister Eckhart (1260–1327), Jacob Boehme (1575–1624), Giordano Bruno (1548–1600), Goethe (1749–1832), William Blake (1757–1827), the early Hegel (1770–1831), the early Marx (1818–1883), C. G. Jung (1875–1962), and in our own time the practitioners of liberation theology in Latin America, such as Gustavo Gutierrez, Miguel Bonino, Leonardo Boff, and Juan Luis Segundo. Most of these pioneers developed their theoretical and practical understanding of transformation in terms of the four faces of our being: personal, political, historical, and sacred. Some practitioners of the countertradition emphasized more faces of our being than others, while some neglected several faces. For example, Marx failed to deal with the personal and sacred faces.

All members of the countertradition came to realize that there are two scenes in act I (as shown in Figure 1); scene 2 is filled with temptation, heresy, doubts, intuitions, and experiences that have their origin in our deepest sources, beyond the official voice of conscience. It is this inner voice that undermines the effectiveness of official repression. Increasingly we suspect that there is something more, an unrealized aspect of our lives, that must be explored. To take these feelings and insights seriously is to make the conscious decision to leave act I, scene 1, and to break with the significant others who have held us there. However, some will make the choice to repress the new and to see those who increase their insecurity as deviants, outsiders, and troublemakers.

Thus to take act I, scene 2 seriously is to enter into act II, scene 1 and to enact the relationship of incoherence wherein we break with our parents and our religious upbringing and begin to contradict, to go against, to counter the established tradition, and to see and enact a different world. Having entered into act II, many arrest their journeys and identify their rebellion and alienation with freedom. Only the particular concrete manifestations of inherited archetypal dramas and ways of relating are consciously rejected; but—like an adolescent ego—the person now feels freed from all previous inhibitions.

This sense of freedom gives way to a feeling of doing whatever one wants but, at the same time, comes a realization that the world is now hostile. Rather than continue their journeys, many begin to create fortresses in a world they do not understand. It is very important to say here that this is not a rational, subjective choice on our part; we have not become "secularized" merely by rejecting the god of emanation. Other sacred forces are present.

The god of incoherence, the god that inspires the pursuit of self-interest and power, does not want us to continue the journey. This god competes with the god of orthodox truth by ridiculing and rejecting the realm of emanation. There is only power and self-interest with no other meaning to life. Yet to choose to remain in this stage of the journey (act II, scene 1) is to be like the man in the scripture who gets rid of the devil and sweeps and cleans his house, believing himself to be secure. Seven other devils return and possess him even more violently than the first. This god is present in the depths but, because the gods are relegated to outmoded superstitions, we can no longer name what drives and obsesses us.

Therefore, we get trapped in systems that possess us and turn us against each other in a perpetual competition that turns our relationships into contests of mutual suspicion and fear. To overcome our vulnerability we seek power, which, of course, increases our fragility. There is no security. We turn this attempt to organize insecurity, without being able to name it, into a whole way of life of incoherence.

There is a further danger in act II. Because we have broken only with our actual mothers and fathers, we remain vulnerable to the lord, to the archetype in the depths that gave our parents their mysterious hold over us. Thus it is not enough to empty ourselves only on the level of the concrete; we must also reject in act II, scene 2 the lord—the archetypal drama and the way of life—that inspired and gave numinous power to our parents. We must now say "No" to the archetype of the father and mother and to the container of emanation. Otherwise, we will merely repeat what we have rejected. We have not really left home because the sacred sources of act I still rule our souls. Living in two acts splits our lives in two so that we are not only fragmented from each other but separated from ourselves. To be caught within and between two acts of the core drama and distinct sacred sources creates a great deal of anxiety and guilt. We know we cannot live the values of the past and yet we feel their pull upon us. At the same time we are aware that we have to protect ourselves in a brutally competitive world.

Owing to the fragility of both of these ways of life, we are tempted to end the impasse by attempting to totally repress the way of life of emanation and to choose power as an end in itself. But to do so is to reject any values inherited from the past that may have made life bearable in a world of brutal power. As a result, in the pursuit of self-interest, anyone who gets in the way becomes not only an enemy but an ultimate threat—ultimate because there is nothing else to life but power. This situation now places people in danger of exiting the journey and of entering into the abyss by consciously choosing to cripple others who threaten their power.

At this point a strange thing happens. To justify why they should have power, those who fear losing power regress to a pseudo form of act I. They want to feel justified in what they are doing without having any moral doubts. But to do this they have to create a false history and identity—an allegedly golden past where everyone knew their place. Because they are of a different color, or are women, or have the wrong faith, they are excluded. Thus the truth now resides only in a fragment that represents the powerful: their gender, race, class, religious beliefs, or other illusion. This fragment, such as skin pigmentation, now becomes the basis for judging the whole of a person's worth. A fantasy, a lie, is manufactured to dominate the whole of life. These are the steps and strategies of deformation that make life fundamentally worse. This strategy constitutes the conscious choice to exit the core drama and to enter into the abyss.

In the way of life of emanation (act I), the powerful often resorted to deformation to defend their world. Those who listened to their inner voices were often killed because they refused to accept a truth given once and for all. But these courageous people pushed the whole society to take the scene 2 of act I seriously and put pressure on others to enter act II as a possibility. Furthermore, they opened up the promise of being able to free themselves and others from the guilt of breaking away by guiding others through act II, scene 2, wherein people can empty themselves of the lords that possessed their souls in act I.

There were five ways by which to treat persons who were not in your container whom you wanted to control and who took the core drama of transformation seriously: (1) they were isolated and made invisible; (2) society made them into pariahs, inferior people who were allowed only to do the menial in life; (3) those judged to be like the superior were adopted as "honorary" members of the elite and thus were allowed to assimilate as a reward for not being like the rest of "those people"; (4) if a person reneged on their loyalty to the dominant elite that gave them privileges, they were cast out, excommunicated; (5) the allegedly inferior could be exterminated by war, exploitation, forced exile, and starvation.

In a strikingly similar manner, Iris M. Young speaks of a similar story when she writes of the five faces of oppression: the marginal, the powerless, the exploited, the victims of cultural imperialism, and those subject to systematic violence.[7] This creation of the archetypal drama of oppression in the service of deformation began as an attempt to preserve the way of life of emanation. Of its very nature this way of life cannot accept fundamentally new consciousness, creativity, new forms of justice, linkages to outsiders, and, most important, that anyone could receive any new inspiration from the depths. To prevent these eruptions of the sacred, more and more force and violence must be used to protect the one "truth."

Those attempting to preserve their power in the way of life of incoherence are also tempted to resort to the drama of oppression as a form of deformation because they believe, in spite of all of their secularism, in a god who made some to be rich and others to be their servants. The irony of this approach is that a group that has cast off the superstitions of its past and that prides itself on its rationality has been possessed by a new sacred force, the lord of deformation. This sacred source of deformation does more than arrest the journey; the whole journey is now put at risk not only for themselves but for all.

The god of transformation is radically different; this lord needs and desires our participation in the fourfold transformation of the sacred, the self, one's neighbor, and the world. To empty ourselves thrice over in act II, scene 2—that is, of our actual concrete father, of the underlying archetype of the father and of the way of life in which a father held one—is to prepare ourselves to be filled anew by the source of sources in act III.

The way of life of transformation and the god of transformation provide the only matrix within which we can express the capacity, freedom, and wholeness of being fully human both in our concrete creation and our sacred depths and thus fully realize love and justice. Like Wagner's Parsifal, we become women and men on a journey who participate in *erlosung dem Erloser*, "saving the Savior" or "redeeming the Redeemer" within ourselves.[8] The source of sources is free to continuously re-create the world only when we are prepared to participate as gods of transformation. We then become the manifestations of gods. We incarnate the god who inspires us, who actually breathes within us.

Nor is this a transformation once for all. The source of sources continues to pour forth creation and invites us to join as cocreators of the universe. The world is imperfect, the source is unfinished, and we are still journeying. Everything is in process; everything is a performance. the first two gods of emanation and incoherence seek to arrest the journey and, in the case of the lord of deformation, to have us exit into the abyss. Our choice is the god who helps us flow, form, and transform—time and again.

ARCHETYPAL ANALYSIS: PARTICIPATING IN THE LIFE AND DEATH OF SACRED SOURCES AND STORIES

Archetypal analysis is grounded on a theory of transformation that allows us to know both the concrete and its origins in underlying patterning sources. To apply and practice this kind of analysis is to become conscious of the full panoply of human capacity and its actualization. This theory helps us to see beyond the concrete, specific realities of our daily lives to comprehend those forming underlying realities known as sacred, or archetypal, forces. An archetype is the necessary form in which all concrete realities manifest themselves. We are constantly enacting archetypes; they move through us and in us.

Thus to do archetypal analysis is to really grasp the underlying meaning of the stories of our lives. This approach is unique in the social sciences in claiming that by the very nature of our humanity all of us share in these sacred depths. But we were never taught that archetypes as sacred sources die and new ones are born. Therefore, we did not know how to free ourselves from the dying and destructive faces of the sacred so that we could participate with other creative gods, such as the transforming god, to grow new and more loving stories. People can struggle against both the destructive, concrete manifestations and the underlying archetypal sources in order to choose and enact more compassionate and just relationships and stories.

To tell archetypal stories or create new ones is to participate in the symbols and journey of transformation. Discovering archetypal stories is more than a story and more than a plot. It is the account of the intertwining of humanity and the divine. To be involved in the creation of stories is to be linked with divine creativity and to participate in the creation, nourishment, and destruction of sacred sources. To reject a particular god, a way of life, or a story of our life is not only to break with an external concrete manifestation but to descend into the deeper depths and to recognize that all of our stories are sacred because the gods are within us, themselves manifestations of the source of all sources, *ein-sof*, or the undifferentiated source (which is usually referred to as God in our society). The gods and the sacred permeate our lives.

If we see theory only as rational categories and abstractions, we miss the real drama in the underlying plane—the life and death of sacred sources, the making and remaking of ultimate meaning. Our task is therefore not to stand by passively as the gods command us but to struggle and wrestle with them until we discern their (and our) true identity.

A THEORY OF HUMAN RELATIONSHIPS ENACTED WITHIN DIFFERENT ARCHETYPAL WAYS OF LIFE

Our analysis is based on a theory of transformation that asserts there is a structure to the universe, the core drama of transformation. The core drama consists of three acts; within the matrix of these three acts we enact archetypal relationships, archetypal ways of life, and the stories of our lives. The theory of transformation sees the encounter between self, other, and the transpersonal with respect to concrete problems as the most fundamental dialectic in human life. According to this view, the quality of the connections between individuals, groups, families, ideas, and our personal and transpersonal sources is what gives us the capacity simultaneously to be free to change yet continue our connections to others, to be able to conflict yet cooperate, and to work toward a more compassionate justice for all.

What constitutes our first worldwide revolution consists precisely in breaking the concrete, inherited manifestations of archetypal relationships and the dying of the way of life of emanation. (Increasingly in our own time the way of life of incoherence is also proving to be fragile as we confront many kinds of problems that cannot be resolved by calculated self-interest.) Everywhere in the world societies and cultures founded on an ultimate truth and ways of doing things as god's will are being undermined and subverted.

The concrete manifestations of inherited archetypal relationships and the way of life of emanation are breaking because they can no longer give us the capacity to respond to the flow of life, to the changes that demand a new kind of self, a renewed relationship to those around us, and a mutual creation with our underlying depths.

Figure 2 is a drawing that provides a symbolic representation of the eight archetypal relationships by which we shape daily life and

Figure 2
Eight Archetypal Relationships and Four Archetypal Ways of Life, Symbolized

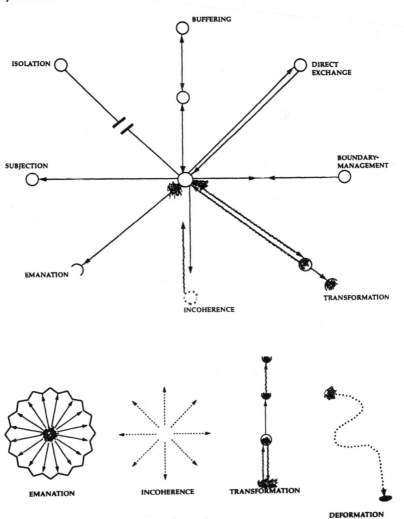

the four ways of life within which we enact these relationships. The top portion of the figure is a mandala symbolizing eight archetypal relationships: emanation, subjection, isolation, buffering, direct exchange, boundary management, incoherence, and transformation. These are the patterns by which we shape daily life and live the stories of our lives. For example, a Latino family living in the way of life of emanation in act I, scene 1 of the core drama is limited to the use of five relationships because, as explained below, these five relationships are the officially sanctioned that sustained and maintained the realm of emanation. We are in difficulty when the concrete, inherited manifestations of these underlying patterns no longer give us the ability to deal with the five issues of daily, human performance: continuity and change, collaboration and conflict, and the just use of resources. Each concrete form of an archetypal relationship gives us a different ability to cope with these five issues of performance.

Usually the repertory of archetypal relationships available to people have been limited by the societies in which they were raised to one dominant and two or three subdominant relationships in dealing with most problems of life. For example, in the container of emanation, youth were socialized to relate to their elders in only five ways: the relationships of emanation, subjection, isolation, buffering, and direct exchange. As we will see, these five patterns of relating provide people with a maximum of continuity and cooperation and shield them from conflict and change. The benefit, or justice, rendered by these relationships is that they provide security but at the cost of not being able to speak about one's own desires if these contradict the society's norms.

These relationships will be fully explained with examples later in this chapter. Our goal is to demystify the concrete, inherited manifestations of these eight archetypal patterns of the Latino family so that when they break, as they increasingly do, people will recognize that they can reject the concrete, inherited manifestations of these underlying patterns and create new concrete combinations of archetypal patterns that restore to Latinos the capacity to change their families. We can identify those patterns that have to be struggled against by naming them clearly as patterns that, in their present concrete form, cripple the human capacity to reexperience self, other, and our creative sources.

However, the eight archetypal relationships, which we will now define and give examples of, do not stand alone. Each of the eight archetypal relationships in their concrete manifestations derive their deeper meaning and value from a wider matrix—a whole way of life, either that of emanation, incoherence, transformation, or deformation (see bottom part of Figure 2). Emanation, incoherence, and transformation as archetypal relationships differ from emanation, incoherence, and transformation as whole ways of life. We will always specify which we mean, the relationship or the overarching, entire way of life.

Each of these ways of life determines the quality of our life; consequently, the eight archetypal relationships are neither negative nor creative in themselves; their quality or ultimate meaning is given to them within the way of life in which we choose to enact them.

No archetypal relationship is ever enacted in and for itself. It gains its larger content, meaning, and purpose by virtue of its contributions to, and derivation from, a larger context. The largest of the contexts—ways at once of asking, seeing, understanding, organizing, working, suffering, and enjoying human relationships—we call archetypal ways of life. Just as it is possible to discover and demonstrate that there are only eight archetypal relationships, so it is also possible to discover and demonstrate that all particular and concrete ways of life in human history are manifestations of four ultimate choices. These are the ways of life of emanation, incoherence, deformation, and transformation. No archetypal relationship can be enacted except in the service of one of these four ways of life.[9]

Having given this introduction, let us now proceed to consider in depth the eight relationships available to us and by which we pattern daily life. Within our discussion of the eight encounters we will also return to the core drama of transformation and of choosing among archetypal dramas enacted within the four ways of life.

What are the archetypal patterns of relationships that link the members of la familia Latina? From one moment to the next, our theory sensitizes us to the realization that a person, a group, a family may be in the process of creation, nourishment, or destruction. Furthermore, the energies released in this perpetual process are given shape by the eight specific archetypal relationships, and given their deeper meaning by the archetypal dramas and the four archetypal ways of life within which we enact relationships. Practiced within a particular drama or way of life, each of our eight archetypal relationships has its own capacity to relate ourselves to self, to the other members of the family, and to problems.

EIGHT ARCHETYPAL RELATIONSHIPS

For all encounters between self and other in all recorded human history and in all societies, there exist only eight different types of relationships which give people the capacity to deal simultaneously with continuity and change, collaboration and conflict, and the achieving of justice. That there are eight and only eight ways applies to all intrapersonal, interpersonal, and intergroup relations. In intergroup relations, it applies to any group, from a family or friendship group to a nation or to the human species as a whole. It also applies to the relationship of individuals and groups to concepts—any concepts of problems, ideas, values, norms, ideology, and the rest. This hypothesis also applies to our connection to those energies which we may call transpersonal, whatever our particular name for them whether we call them the unconscious, the sacred, or god.[10]

Let us now proceed to an explanation of the eight forms of encounter and four ways of life. We will begin with the limited repertory of five relationships enacted within the way of life of emanation that constitute what I call the inherited Latino model.

Emanation

This is an encounter in which one treats the other solely as an extension of one's self. The other accepts the denial of his/her own separate identity because of the mysterious and overwhelming power of the source of this emanation—a yielding which is rewarded with total security. All of us began life as children without power adequate to meet the other. We therefore necessarily yielded our identity to the mysterious and overwhelming power of our mother until we freed ourselves to risk losing total security. However, some fathers or mothers seek to retain all members of their household as emanations of themselves. Others treat their property or their employees in this way. Many individuals remain eager to submerge themselves as emanations of another—of a political movement, a dogma or a lover.[11]

The relationship of emanation is the most prevalent relationship even in the time in which we live. It points out an unexamined, unconscious, uncritical relationship to a mysterious and overwhelming source that contains us and within which we live our inherited stories. Indeed we are not even conscious of archetypal dramas. We may see emanation manifested in the Latina who sees herself as an extension of husband and family; the worker who acts solely as the expression of the supervisor's personality without any autonomous jurisdiction of his or her own. Also we see emanation manifested in the believer as the embodiment of the Catholic *carismaticos* or Protestant Pentecostals, two groups that often compete with each other to provide a more secure container for Latinos set adrift in our urban centers.

It is an intensely passive collaboration at the cost of repressing conflict, a willingness to purchase continuity by implicitly accepting or rejecting change solely at the behest of another, and hence granting mysterious and overwhelming power to the one in exchange for total security for the other.[12] It means remaining firmly ensconced in act I, scene 1 of the core drama of transformation.

Subjection

Here both self and other are fully present, but in reality both are denied a full presence and an identity of his/her own. The relationship is still asymmetrical; it still rests upon the experience of overwhelming power. But this power, which was mysterious in emanation, becomes naked in subjection—naked in its source, imposition, and resistance.[13]

We see subjection in the European-Americans displacing the Californios from their land by legal trickery and beatings; the teacher demanding that Latino children speak English at all times; the Latino father or husband solely controlling the spending of the family's finances; the U.S. Navy continuing to use Vieques, Puerto Rico, for naval and aerial maneuvers involving the use of testing weaponry with live ammunition. Subjection, in our special use of this term, can also be exemplified by the use of instrumental rationality. Subjection exists whenever someone controls others as a means to their own end, whether they base this control on the naked power of the logic of deductive reasoning, on standards of efficiency or economy, or simply on the power of the gun.

In subjection, conflict is no longer repressed but suppressed. Latinos remain conscious of the loss of their right to step forward
urgently and freely. Collaboration is based on explicit rules defined
solely by the dominant world. But the majority of Latinos were
also controlled in Latin America before migrating to the United
States. Latino *caudillos* or *jefes* (bosses) often combined emanation
and subjection when relating to peasants or laborers. Thus Latinos
were prepared to relate to authority figures in this country with the
same deference and respect given in Latin America. The dominant
group therefore assures continuity and change in accordance with
their power. Justice involves an exchange of the right of survival
for the one in exchange for his or her acceptance of the supremacy
of power of the other. Many times Latinos survived by giving up
their right to create conflict or change on their own.

Buffering

This encounter is managed by intermediaries. Such a position may be
occupied by a mediator, broker, or by a concept. Buffering allows for
change by permitting indirect, intermittent, or segmented forms of conflict
and collaboration.[14]

Among Latinos, the use of mediators in the family, like a *padrino*
or *madrina* (godparents), is common; so is the use of the parish
priest (*el cura*) to arrange marriages and secure other advantages.
Saints, and especially *La Virgen*, may be asked to intercede. Ritu-
alistic language, such as *Ay Bendito!* (Oh, Good Lord!), *Queriendo
Dios* (God willing), *Ni lo mande Dios* (May God forbid), may be
used to ease moments of change. In all societies buffering is perhaps
most often exemplified by mediating one's own experiences through
a filter of habits and stereotypes. Justice in buffering is obtaining
some change and conflict that achieves a certain amount of self-
determination through the intervention of a third party. The problem here is that our freedom relies on the ability and skill of the
mediator; and therefore our self-determination is limited and we
remain dependent on others. In Latino families, as in many others,
the mother becomes an institutionalized buffer who often uses a
good meal to prepare the father for bad news, such as threats to

his authority from a daughter who wants to attend college and live in a dorm away from home.

Isolation

Isolation was available as an acceptable relationship by which to deal with the issues of daily life.

In this relationship, individuals or groups agree upon one mode of collaboration—to refrain from demanding anything of each other. Both sides here collaborate in avoiding all conflict intended to lead to change in, with, or by the other. Justice, in contrast to emanation and subjection, means self-determination—but at the price of not attempting to affect change in the others. Isolation in this use of the term cannot be achieved unilaterally. It demands collaboration. The attempt to isolate without an agreement to avoid conflict, change, or new forms of justice produces incoherence, not isolation.[15]

Latino men in the way of life of emanation could physically withdraw and do as they pleased so that wives felt themselves agreeing not to confront them to avoid conflict or change. As a matter of fact, the granting of such freedom to physically withdrawal to men and not to women meant that isolation was used to enforce a woman's condition of dependency. A woman could also practice isolation but only psychologically by being present but inaccessible to her husband who at times might wonder what she might be thinking. A woman was allowed some inner psychic space and demonstrated this through periods of moodiness, a sense of stoic forbearance, or just being silent and withdrawn. The different use of isolation by men and women underlines a structural inequality. Although men could withdraw both physically and psychically, women for the most part could practice only an internal isolation. But as we will see later in the book, women used their psychic isolation to eventually help break the patriarchal container in the way of life of emanation that had prevented them from enacting isolation in the service of transformation.

Direct Exchange

In this form of encounter, individuals and groups conflict and collaborate with each other directly. Justice is not only the better bargain that may accrue to one side or the other, but above all the reciprocal capacity to seek a different bargain as, from moment to moment, the balance of power changes.[16]

By means of gifts or favors, Latinos often create or maintain a sense of indebtedness between self and other. Or they follow a form of rebellion that is in fact a continuance of this encounter—that is, when one remains angrily present while refusing to bargain precisely in order to improve one's bargaining position. A wife, for example, remains silent but bangs dishes until her husband relents and allows her to do what she has requested. In this way anger is reduced to catharsis so that real change can be avoided because the husband gave his permission; this is system-maintaining change.

Whether the demand be for submission to the will of one's father, lover, or god, each Latino usually exercised only five choices in the service of emanation, arrested in act I, scene 1. This was a limited repertory that excluded the use of the other three relationships of autonomy, incoherence, and transformation and the two ways of life of incoherence and transformation. These three relationships and two ways of life were forbidden in the way of life of emanation.

Thus within their inherited repertory of relationships Latinos could entirely give themselves up—to the best of their power for yielding—to becoming an emanation or extension of the mysterious and overwhelming power of father, lover, or the sacred. Or, they could subject themselves in deliberate response measured to the displayed power of the other. Or, a Latina woman could bargain directly with the god or emanation, no less than husband or father, saying in each case: in return for my submission, I expect something for my good behavior or I will not cease my aggravation without some kind of reward. Or, if one possessed neither the power to bargain, nor the will to submit or to give themselves totally, they could resort to buffering—ask their mother-in-law to mediate with her son, or say the rosary to intercede with *La Virgen*, use rose water with sugar to expel evil spirits, or use amulets to filter out *el mal ojo* (the evil eye). Or they could recede into a silent isolation.

This was the repertory within the way of life of emanation in which many Latinos were raised; these were the linkages available to them in the uncritically inherited Latino world of act I, scene 1. However, there is no doubt that Spain's Conquest of Latin America and later the coming of the market economy, brought massive breakdown for the indigenous peoples. They had already experienced the trauma of not knowing who they were or of the direction of the world. Many, but certainly not all, attempted to put the world back together by taking the story of the Spaniards as their own. Therefore, what held the whole world together, even though much more tenuously for the Native American population, was the overarching way of life of emanation made up of two similar cosmologies: the indigenous and Catholic/Christian hierarchies. In both worlds there was a clear chain of emanation that linked them to one common source, the divine. From that source emanated the authority that legitimized the link between ruled and ruler, husband and wife, child and parent.

THE WAY OF LIFE OF EMANATION: THE
INHERITED WAY OF LIFE OF *LA FAMILIA LATINA*

The deeper and larger context within which Latinos lived the stories of their lives and enacted their repertory of five relationships was the way of life of emanation, arrested in act I, scene 1 of the core drama of transformation.

Politics in the service of emanation (for example, in the service of a fixed faith or tradition) holds us within containers in which all we can and need to do together is already codified and ritualized, and declared to be no longer a problem except for the skill and intensity with which we affirm, elaborate, deepen or refine what we are already performing together. Emanation is a way of life in which a moment of truth has become frozen, distorted, or corrupted. This way of life of politics is everywhere in the world being questioned and undermined.[17]

Any attempt to leave the way of life of emanation arrested in act I, scenes 1 or 2 means breaking with the inherited concrete manifestations and underlying archetypal relationships in such a way that it will lead to a change of relationships for self and others. This is clearly heresy and dangerous to a cosmos blessed once and for all by the god of emanation. In the past people were killed for such thoughts and behavior, which appeared to the orthodox to be the demonic come to life. It has always been dangerous for people living in closed societies to practice the heresy of contacting the sacred so as to participate in continual creation. Life for most Latinos was arrested in act I of the core drama as god's will.

Latino traditional society was never dull or boring. Each Latino always differed in the specific ways in which they expressed these archetypal relations. From one moment to the next a person was bargaining for a better deal, seeking a friend to mediate with a mutual acquaintance, hoping to find security through attaching themselves to a more powerful source of mystery, a saint or patron, withdrawing into moodiness, or simply surviving by standing in line for hours to get employment, better benefits, or to buy a necessary license.

At times, wives reversed the relations of emanation not only in the bedroom and kitchen but permanently in all areas of life such that their husbands lost their honor among macho males. Some wives also succeeded in physically dominating their husbands so that they needed mediators to protect them. Or as my own mother said when my father died, "Now I have to be both your father and mother." Many of us from single-parent families learned to see our mothers as the real source of mystery. These relationships were always acceptable because they were ultimately sanctioned by the god of emanation. The whole of the repertory was in the service of the way of life of emanation, a web of life blessed with divine sanction.

In the following pages, we will be looking more closely at the Latina women's limited repertory and some of the archetypal dramas, especially that of the patriarchal family and possessive male/female relationships, which will allow us to see actual daily behavior. We will go beyond mere descriptions of the breaking of the concrete and inherited manifestations of these five archetypal relationships and the dying way of life of emanation, and the rejection of certain sacred dramas to consider how we might transform such incoherence. However, as long as the inherited repertory of relationships in the service of emanation, in act I of the core drama, remained in effect, both in Latin America and here in the United States, Latinos did not have the ability to cope with continuity and change, collaboration and conflict, with a justice of security. They remained limited and partial selves who could not respond to new problems.

Many Latinos, in order to assure continuity after migrating to the United States, transferred their loyalty from the Catholic Church in their native country to that of the U.S. Catholic Church. For the time being, the Catholic Church provided an important source of emanational fiber to help to provide some security in the midst of great upheaval.

But what the church could not do was restore the original web of life experienced in Latin America with all of its meaning and security. Too often even the church saw its duty as helping Latinos assimilate into the mainstream of U.S. society *without* having dealt with the cultural incoherence of Latino people. The church, like official bilingual programs, saw its role as helping Latinos to be assimilated. Latinos were just another immigrant group to accommodate. This is why the Catholic Church has had such ambivalent feelings about Latino resistance to U.S. culture.

THE FORBIDDEN REPERTORY OF RELATIONSHIPS AND WAYS OF LIFE

All societies, or the body politic, shape our ego. Through socialization the community introduces us to the *acceptable* repertory of concrete forms of the eight archetypal relationships. That is to say that not all eight forms of our archetypal relationships are seen as positive options. Consequently, people are forbidden to choose ways of life and to enact certain relationships; often we are not even aware of the existence of alternatives. The same is true for the archetypal dramas and archetypal ways of life that are available to us. In U.S. society the archetypal way of life, which we are all led to believe and accept as natural, is that of incoherence, the legitimation of the pursuit of self-interest.

In the inherited way of life of Latinos, the ways of life of incoherence and transformation (which will be fully explained later) were forbidden. The relationships that were excluded were those of autonomy, incoherence, and transformation. The way of life of incoherence dominant in U.S. society caused fear and withdrawal. Transformation as a way of life was seldom known or practiced. The way of life of deformation has become more frequent as some Latino families fail to cope with the growing incoherence. So let us now consider in depth the excluded relationships and the ways of life.

Boundary Management

This is an encounter in which each self and other is entitled to claim an autonomous zone of jurisdiction based on some explicit principle of law, custom, status, value, or competence that both share. The individual or group whose zone of autonomy has been effectively reduced may as a consequence have to consider changing behavior.... Justice in the encounter of boundary management is the reciprocal right of each to sustain or enlarge their autonomous zone of jurisdiction. Boundary management is the form of encounter which allows us to be fellow-citizens, to separate yet keep in constant tension the three branches of government, ... to create autonomy yet collaboration among professions, scholarly disciplines, and bureaucracies. The encounter of boundary management allows large numbers of individuals and groups to collaborate on a sustained basis in connected roles, for each claim can be challenged in order to be joined or subdivided, or a principle found to add more connections in the chain.[18]

Boundary management in the service of incoherence on the personal level demands aggressive, calculating individuals who know how to advance their interests by enlarging their area of jurisdiction or who know when to defend their zone of autonomy against another bureaucrat who seeks to redraw the area under his jurisdiction to include yours. The relationship of boundary management on the societal level is the relationship enacted when the rights of Mexicans to work and live in the United States are involved. The whole question of undocumented persons is a question of two autonomous jurisdictions, Mexico and the United States, stating those rights within their own borders. On the personal level, it entails a skilled professional with competence relating to clients. Or in a family, intent upon being fully assimilated into the way of life of incoherence in act II, scene 1, it means the relationship between a husband and wife or parents and children who have certain autonomous rights based on explicit contractual principles. For example, the wife has her own day off and money to spend; children have the right to lock their rooms and to an allowance.

Latino parents, raised in the way of life of emanation, accurately saw such a relationship as a threat to their authority and demand for uncritical loyalty as a form of respect. Latinos, especially from the rural areas of Latin America, did not, on the whole, practice the relationship of boundary management in the family nor in the greater society and, therefore, have had great difficulties in adjusting to U.S. society. Furthermore, in the public realm, working with strangers to achieve a common goal by forming organizations such as unions or school associations was almost totally foreign to them. The lack of the relationship of boundary management helps to explain why Latinos seem reluctant to work together.

Puerto Ricans, Chicanos, Dominicans, Cubans, Colombians, Peruvians, and other Latino groups are being asked to cooperate with each other and other non-Latino groups even though they were strangers and even though they have never participated in large-scale, sustained, autonomous, and coordinated public institutions such as a labor union that works on explicit legal principles and that allows the members to protect themselves against large corporations. Labor unions may in fact be corrupted from within by bosses who undermine the original democratic nature of the union and run it on relationships of emanation, as a personal fiefdom, or as a thugdom ruled by subjection. But unions do carry the potential to be used positively as an organization to achieve a just participation in the fruits of one's labor such as Cesar Chavez and the United Farm Workers have proven.

As Latinos our lack of the knowledge and use of the relationship of boundary management helps to explain why for so long Latinos were cheated when it came to contracts, accepting vague promises based on the good character of the salesperson who had earned their *confianza* (confidence). They were seduced temporarily into the old repertory where honor and one's good word linked persons in a common emanational web of life. In a world ruled by concrete inherited manifestations of boundary management and subjection enacted in the service of incoherence, Latinos cannot count on the good intentions of the seller or landlord. Now we have to learn to demand explicit principles that guarantee our rights in a written contract. Many still feel embarrassed demanding these kinds of business relations because we still like to believe that the other is honorable and upholds the same values that we do. So to ask for it in writing is like a *falta de respeto*, or to treat salespersons disrespectfully. Those who are *aprovechandose*, or taking advantage of the situation, realize this hesitation and exploit it.

Incoherence

One of the decisive ways by which the way of life of emanation was arrested in act I and became a permanent container is that it prohibited the relationship of incoherence. You could change and create conflict but only *within* the limits of the orthodox repertory of archetypal relationships—emanation, subjection, isolation, buffering, and direct exchange. But some Latinos were willing to face the stigma of being *sin verguenzas* (people without shame) by shattering the socially acceptable relationships and thereby creating the relationship of incoherence.

Incoherence in our theory is that form of encounter in which self and other face each other in the same place and at the same time but are unwilling or unable to agree upon how, simultaneously, to manage continuity and change, collaboration and conflict, and the achieving of justice between them. Incoherence is not a residual category for purpose of classification, but obviously an experiential alternative to the other forms of encounter. It is the experience of discontinuities rather than continuity; of change, yes, but unintended, uncontrolled change; of conflict without shared rules leading to injustice for both self and others.[19]

Now persons stand face to face, no longer knowing how to relate to each other.

Latino fathers, living in a repertory endowed with the blessing of the god of emanation in act I, scene 1, believed that it was their right to physically discipline children who were considered to have lost respect *because* they enacted new relationships. To introduce boundary management as a relationship between parents and children was to directly threaten the inherited Latino repertory of relationships endowed with emanational mystery and to fundamentally change the Latino family. This was totally unacceptable and incomprehensible. Thus this inability to be able to relate to one another in mutually shared relationships leads to the relationship of incoherence.

Unmarried Latina women, who sought privacy through isolation and personal freedom through enacting the relationship of boundary management by moving to an apartment, from the perspective of the way of life of emanation, were considered to have dishonored the family and thereby created incoherence: father and daughter standing in the presence of each other and being unable to agree on which relationship to use. To heed one's inner voice in act I, scene 2 was to enter into rebellion in act II, scene 1: you break with the person with whom you were previously linked in emanation in act I, scene 1. The only *legitimate* way to leave home was to be handed over from one emanational container, the family, to another new family, the husband and marriage. This meant, from the perspective of the core drama, that a woman never really left her father in act I, but simply married her husband/father and remained in act I. Many knew what they were doing and made a conscious decision to repress their own voice in the second scene of act I in order to remain in scene 1 as a mere extension of their husbands' lives.

It is this kind of repression that allowed the archetypal story of the patriarchy to continue through the generations. Latino fathers prayed for the day when they could successfully (meaning, with virginal status) hand over their precarious charge to an acceptable alternate. He was made acceptable by the buffering role of the priest who gave his blessing as a kind of divine matchmaker. This whole process also ensured the continuity in the souls of the newly married of the archetypal drama of the patriarchal family.

To leave home without this ritualized process was truly an act of incoherence; it was a sin from the perspective of the way of life of emanation. Some daughters used this fear of incoherence as a way of increasing their bargaining power, so that when they did consent to remain at home, more benefits would be granted. But many never came home again, in the sense of returning to the old repertory. All of the psychic artillery of sin, shame, and guilt was used to attempt to restore a woman to her senses. The daughters, and sometimes the sons, insisted that they still loved their parents but in a new way. The parents argued that if you love me, come home again, back to the "normal" way things used to be in act I, scene 1, the dying way of life of emanation.

The result is to speak past one another; persons are now relating in different worlds and mean fundamentally different realities in their use of the word love. What accounts for this is that they are now living in different ultimate ways of life and in different acts of the core drama. The relationships of emanation, subjection, isolation, buffering, and direct exchange enacted in the service of emanation are broken and to the repertory was added the forbidden relationships of boundary management, incoherence, and transformation.

The Forbidden Way of Life of Incoherence. The relationship of incoherence breaks open the way of life of emanation arrested in act I, scenes 1 and 2. But if the relationship of incoherence, which was necessary to polarize the members of the family frozen in inherited patterns, becomes permanently arrested in act II, scene 1, it then becomes another way of shaping life, the way of life of incoherence. The relationship of incoherence, standing in the presence of your loved ones and not knowing what to say or how to relate, is intended to open up new possibilities to travel through the core drama in order to achieve a new kind of wholeness and life. However, if they remain permanently fixed in their anger, then the polarization initiated by the relationship of incoherence becomes arrested as a whole way of life, the way of life of incoherence. In this way of life the person feels increasingly vulnerable in a world of fragmented individuals who feel no commitment to one another. This is a drama, a way of life, that holds together as a story of institutionalized rebellion.

Politics in the service of incoherence takes account of the fact that in the modern age, all our concrete inherited forms of relationships are breaking, but therefore builds fortresses in a desert it cannot overcome. The guardians who would contain us within these fragments insist upon removing much of what we can and need to do together from what they define as politics. They treat politics solely as an arena for contests of power. They seek to give their histories the appearance of final legitimacy (as if they were the true heirs of faith and tradition) in order to justify the exclusion from this arena of all fundamentally new issues and encounters which do not serve their already established power. Hence they compel most people to accept politics as the acknowledgment of dependency upon the powerful and to deny the value and importance of their own miseries and joys.[20]

When the inherited, concrete manifestations of the Latino repertory of relationships, emanation, subjection, isolation, buffering, and direct exchange enacted in the service of the way of life of emanation increasingly lose their ability to shape daily life, especially in the urban centers of Latin America as well as in the United States, the relationship of incoherence begins to dominate their lives. Incoherence means that a person stands in the presence of her way of life, her culture, her relatives, and her self and can no longer relate in the expected manner according to inherited patterns. But rather than allow the relationship of incoherence to lead to a fundamentally new and more loving way by entering scene 2 of act II, in order to empty herself of destructive, inherited archetypal stories, she now settles for less, learns to live with incoherence, arrests the core drama in act II, scene 1, and thereby turns the relationship of incoherence into the overarching drama of incoherence.

The relationship of incoherence in the way of life of emanation was always a sin because it constituted a rejection of the final revelation of the truth. In the way of life of incoherence we have entered into a whole new drama or story of our life. This is a story that holds together around the reality of constant rebellion and insecurity. We cannot count on any absolute meaning or the loyalty of anyone. The past is regarded as superstitious, powerless, old-fashioned, or foolish. To become an American one must become like the dominant group and accept its values, especially the pursuit of power, which arrests Latinos in act II of the core drama. Thus, assimilation as a form of rebellion against the inherited Latino past dominated by emanation moves Latinos into the way of life of incoherence.

Some Latinos created themselves into upwardly mobile, aggressive individuals. Assimilated Latinos who think like the powerful living in the way of life of incoherence become like them in such a way that they are cut off from their own selfhood, fellow Latinos, sister Latinas, and sacred sources. It is important to say here that not all European-Americans live in the service of incoherence. We must not stereotype any group, since in all groups there are individuals who are living and enacting relationships in all four ways of life. Nevertheless, "to make it" is the new heaven, the goal of this kind of metamorphosis. Assimilated Latinos are taken over by a new way of life, that of incoherence. Power becomes the mysterious and overwhelming source of life when life is arrested in act II, scene 1.

This loss of self and the accompanying rejection of others and their own sacred sources is really to live with incoherence, arrested in act II of the core drama. Some Latinos have rejected the old god of emanation but have actually been repossessed by a new god, the god of incoherence. The system based on power became the new god but it possesses just as powerfully as the old god of emanation, only now without the same sense of security; the only certainty now is the insecurity of knowing that nothing is secure or lasting. Since in this way of life we cannot know or acknowledge any ultimate meaning or value or love, one has to get what they can while the going is good. This anxiety feeds a constant need to compete. Success is always limited to organizing the incoherence so that the powerful can protect their right to become more powerful fragments. There is no way out of this story unless we turn the relationship of incoherence into an opportunity to break connections with the story of power and to create the fundamentally more compassionate and just by practicing transformation. In this way incoherence becomes the necessary step toward transformation.

Living Between Two Worlds and Different Ways of Life. Many Latino immigrants were overwhelmed by change and conflict. There was often only the justice of survival in a hostile land. For these reasons, *barrios* were a welcome island of relief from the daily onslaught. But they were islands of emanational security, fragments of the dying way of life of emanation, providing some refuge when all else was breaking. Many attempted to continue the way of life lived in Puerto Rico, El Salvador, Chile, or Mexico. This is why *compadrazgo,* or creating a network of comothers and cofathers (godparents) for children was so important. Godparents, especially if they were better off financially, became new sources of emanation and buffering in a confusing world.

The continuity of the old world in the midst of the new really meant an attempt to hang on to a way of life blessed by the god of emanation. The world outside the *barrio,* as little as a block or an alley away, represented a forbidden world, the way of life of incoherence representing different values and patterns of relating, a world signifying temptation and sin. This living between two worlds created a disconnected and fragmented way of life for most Latinos. They were now somewhat consciously living between the acceptable and forbidden relationships and two overarching ways of life: the ways of life of emanation and incoherence.

Parents lost much of their authority in this dual existence: living act I of the world of emanation and the world of incoherence in act II. Many parents, to cover their own sense of loss in the way of life of incoherence in the public realm, demanded a total loyalty at home, hanging on to the inherited relationships and the dying way of life of emanation. Resistance by a daughter or son was met by appeals to loyalty in emanation, demands for obedience as in subjection, mediation by godparents or friends as in buffering, or direct exchange to offer incentives for staying in the container (the way of life of emanation).

But unlike the *rancho* there was another world beyond the doorsteps that provided a whole other repertory of relationships in competition with the concrete inherited forms of emanation, subjection, buffering, isolation and direct exchange. The dominant world offered boundary management, both personally and socially for both women and men; the right to be left alone in isolation, physically as well as psychologically; increased bargaining power through education, with new buffers such as teachers and counselors; boyfriends; a new identity as an American; together with symbols of success, portrayed daily in the media. With these options available, it became increasingly difficult to maintain the viability of the inherited repertory and way of life of emanation and the archetypal drama of the patriarchal family.

Rebellion was no longer just a ploy to get a better deal in the family and therefore end by restoring and strengthening the inherited repertory; rebellion was now far more serious because the threat to punish the child who did not obey or the pregnant daughter or the angry wife might end with them never returning. This situation created more and more the relationship of incoherence: two people standing in the presence of one another not knowing what to say or how to relate to each other. The breaking of connections was played out in countless homes throughout the Latino community.

So instead of changes *within* the available repertory there was now the threat of changes *of* the repertory, which meant choosing a new set of relationships previously forbidden by the emanational world arrested in act I, and entering into a new way of living in the way of life of incoherence in act II, that legitimized new relationships so that parents, husband, or lover could no longer dominate. This brought about the confusion of being caught in two competing ways of life and simultaneously living in two acts of the core drama, neither of which provided much help.

Transformation

The relationship of transformation is an encounter in which one's consciousness is no longer the mere embodiment of an external source of
emanation but has become conscious of those sources in the depths which
constitute the archetypal dramas and stories of our lives. To enact this
relationship is to keep alive a conscious awareness of alternative dramas
of relationship being created, nourished, petrified, destroyed, or recreated;
a creativity that empowers us to be acted upon as well as to act, and thus
woo new combinations into being; a linking with others that is at once
knowing and loving; a justice which is participation in becoming and
being.[21]

Latinas who create a new sense of self, break inherited relationships, and reject in act II, scene 2 the archetypal dramas in the
service of emanation and incoherence that possessed their souls,
create new linkages to others previously forbidden to them, and
create alternative stories of their life based on mutuality have enacted the drama of transformation. In act III, scene 1 people are
inspired by a new vision of how to shape life anew. In scene 2 of
act III, this new intuition is actually put into practice. One of the
results of this newfound wholeness is that it enables people to enact
not only all eight relationships but an infinite number of concrete
manifestations of each relationship. This is what is meant to participate in the process of create, nourish, and destroy in order to
create time and again.

However, what looks like transformation can be distorted because it is in reality reformation. Transformation in the service
of emanation is not possible; the very logic of emanation as a
way of life precludes the emergence of the fundamentally new as
a form of the worst heresy. Change that may be called transformation is reformation when a person alters their personality but
in order to be more loyal to their lover, church, hero, or mother.
Transformation is frustrated as reformation in the way of life of
emanation when a Latina becomes the first doctor in her family's
history but she herself did not choose to practice medicine and
became a doctor only to remain loyal to her parents' wishes.

This is not a transformation but one that was performed in response to the question: How can I ultimately show uncritical loyalty
to mysterious others? Such a person is really arrested in act I, scene

2 since she was inspired to become someone new but then she responded in this scene of the core drama by becoming a better extension of someone else. Transformation always means the creation of the fundamentally more loving and just alternatives in all aspects of our life. Transformation will be further discussed as a whole way of life later in this chapter.

EXITING THE CORE DRAMA: THE WAY OF LIFE
OF DEFORMATION

In discussing the way of life of deformation as the exit from the core drama of transformation, I would like to return to the context of the family in incoherence.

Appeals to honor, authority, respect, and legitimized subjection no longer have their intended effect, because the ways of life of emanation and incoherence are so fragile. The whole of life from the perspective of the core drama is intended to be a persistent process of creation. Therefore incoherence in the family arrested in either acts I or II is bound to increase through the experience of broken connections that previously bound them together. For example, the father or mother, once considered unquestionable sources of emanation who ruled with god's blessing, no longer provide for their children an overwhelming sense of security. Efforts to return to the way of life of emanation fail; the new relationships of official U.S. society are rejected by the patriarchal *familia Latina* but are embraced by some members of the family.

Some parents and spouses decide that there is only one way: the use of physical, psychic, or financial violence to force the errant wife or children to return to the old ways. But a wife or children cannot go back to a container that is now demystified; the subjection previously exercised and blessed by god, because it was part of the legitimacy of the way of life of emanation, is now considered illegitimate. In act I, in the service of emanation, the benefits of believing that you deserve the punishment, given the rules of the game that were broken and accepted by all, restored you to good standing in the family and the proper order of things.

Now, however, this cosmic view has collapsed so that what was once considered acceptable is now seen as unbearable and unacceptable. But it should also be said here that violence was always an acceptable part of the strategy to preserve the way of life of emanation. Therefore deformation as a way of life was available as an ally to attempt to maintain the container of emanation. Wives were beaten as a matter of right for men. It was not necessary for a woman to be in open rebellion to be struck. The greatest and ever growing danger in these circumstances is that the hidden resentment of the father or mother or both will erupt in an irrational manner in the form of violence. The violence might be inner directed so that a father turns to drugs or alcohol to drown his anxiety. Or he might turn to child abuse and battering his wife.

This is deformation because it makes life fundamentally worse. Due to the frustration in his inability to hold the container of emanation together in a new and hostile culture, and because his ego is so closely related to life in act I in the service of emanation, a father, a husband, or a lover may turn toward the abyss of violence and thereby exit the core drama.

A person caught in this descent is painfully aware that something is wrong, but does not know what to do except to try to restore what has been lost. The refusal to go forward through the core drama exposes the wounded nature of being a partial self. Partial selves are essentially people who have arrested their lives in the truncated ways of life of emanation and incoherence. People living within these ways of life are constantly living on the edge of the abyss. Why is this so? Because when act I is arrested as the way of life of emanation, people must guard against any new inspirations from the depths because this way of life tells them there can be nothing new under the sun. Since we cannot escape our unconscious, the underlying realm of sacred sources, this attempt to prevent the emergence of the fundamentally new has failed and will continue to fail.

A person dedicated to this arrested way of living cannot allow any new feelings within themselves nor in those around them. People must continue to repress, deny, and destroy new ideas, feelings, intuitions, and stories that question their way of life. The logic of this means that people are constantly prepared to violate themselves and others in order to keep their family and world intact. This inability to acknowledge crucial aspects of their lives is what constitutes the danger of being a partial self. In order to preserve a stunted identity in a truncated world, the road to violence opens up again and again. For this reason to question is seen as an act of disloyalty that demands a swift retaliation.

In regard to the core drama, those who remain arrested in acts I or II due to loyalty or the desire for power are profoundly threatened by those others who do not accept or who are excluded from participating in the life of the society. In act II, arrested as the drama of incoherence, the greatest fear is the loss or inability to gain power. Anyone who gets in our way is expendable. Power by its very nature, cannot be shared. This drama possesses our soul such that we are not free to be compassionate or loving.

The fragility of uncritical loyalty in the way of emanation and the obsessive pursuit of power in the service of incoherence tempts the true believers and the powerful toward increased violence. This makes life fundamentally worse and turns history downward into the abyss.

Latino families also face the reality of deformation in the public realm. Latino families often live at the lower socioeconomic levels of society. The number of teenage addicts, children born with AIDS, school dropouts, the unemployed, and the homeless is growing at an alarming rate in the Latino community. Fully 39 percent of all Latino children in the United States live in poverty. Latina women and Latino men are becoming an endangered species.

This points to the impact of the wider society's structures and attitudes that cause serious violence to the Latino family. Some of this destructive behavior is a suicidal rebellion against the violence of the drama of tribalism: being excluded from proper housing, education, employment, and access to health facilities. It is very difficult to measure to what extent the family is collapsing from within because of the dying way of life of emanation and to what extent the harm is being done by the powerful in the service of incoherence and the deformative violence of the external society. What is clear is that it is because of both the internal collapse and the external assault. A society permeated by the ways of life of incoherence and deformation creates an environment conducive to turning people into faceless beings who often respond with violence to assert their presence.

THE WAY OF LIFE OF TRANSFORMATION

The way of life of transformation is the most crucial drama of the universe of human relations. The other ways of life are truncated fragments of the core drama that cannot provide us with the necessary vision, imagination, or creativity to respond to our problems. To live in the service of transformation is to persist in continuous creation of the fundamentally new and more loving by journeying through the core drama again and again. The structure of the universe makes sense only if there is a source of the fundamentally more just and compassionate.

The fundamentally new and better cannot come from frozen, orthodox religious institutions and their gods because they have spoken once and for all. We must point to the god beyond god, the source of all sacred sources, and to the only god, the lord of transformation, which can guide us in order to shape and form a more compassionate and inclusive world. Our participation as sons and daughters of the sacred or, indeed, as gods of transformation ourselves, is necessary to transform the personal, political, historical, and sacred faces of our lives. The god of transformation is the only sacred source that has full access to *ein-sof*. The transforming source as our guide gives us access to the source of sources.

Acting in the service of transformation in act III, scene 2 of the core drama means rejecting the inherited and assimilated stories of uncritical loyalty, power, and deformation in our lives so that we might choose the story of life: creating and nourishing fundamentally new and better relationships. To journey through the core drama of transformation is the vocation to which all of us are called. Anyone who prevents this journey for themselves or for others violates a sacred process. A decisive breakthrough has been accomplished when we realize that our greatest freedom is that we can become conscious of the different dramas and relationships in which archetypal forces manifest themselves and prepare ourselves to choose some and reject others and even participate in creating new archetypal stories. This kind of participation can take place only in act III, scenes 1 and 2. In this last act of the core drama of transformation we are empowered as individuals to cooperate with the source of all sources in order to share in the continuous work of creation.

THE FOUR FACES OF OUR BEING: PERSONAL, POLITICAL, HISTORICAL, AND SACRED

The process of transformation takes place first of all in the individual's depths; the archetypal source that crippled us and used our ego as its incarnation is now personally rejected in act II, scene 2 so that we are prepared to be renewed by the sources. But each of us as a person has four faces: personal, political, historical, and sacred. Thus when we reject a particular father or lover or ruler there is a political dimension. Our ego, which also incarnates the body politic—the archetypal way of life that shapes the meaning and purpose of both our personal and political history—therefore says no not only to a person but to the official story of that society.

Therefore we cannot settle for personal transformation. We have to reach beyond our personal lives to the political and historical networks that severely limit our capacity. To resist the racism in one's personal life requires also a struggle against structural deformation in the society that continues to cripple others and to threaten the tenuous personal liberation achieved. We must be political by asking the question: What do we need to do together to liberate ourselves and others from the dramas of control and power that are justified in the wider society in the concrete and in the depths by sacred forces? To cast out demons in society and history means to create a new turning point by struggling with both the immediate concrete tyranny and its underlying forming source and ultimate ways of life.

STRATEGIES OF TRANSFORMATION

By rejecting the inherited ways of life and the stories of our lives we enter into the relationship of incoherence in act II, scene 1, and we break with the official personal, political, historical, and sacred faces of our being. But we cannot create a new history or politics once and for all. This is the failure of utopian politics. Although we have experienced transformation in regard to a particular problem, we will have to make this choice again and again as new problems emerge. This prevents us from stereotyping, from establishing a new orthodoxy, or from declaring that the revolution has been won. We cannot stereotype because at every moment we must test each relationship, each drama and ask finally: in the service of what way of life am I helping to give concrete form to these archetypal forces? It follows from this that no previous incarnation will be authentic once and for all; we must persistently choose, nourish, break, and create so that we can shape life anew.

Authentic self-love means loving others as oneself. Our neighbors and family members might still be largely involved in the fragments of the crippled way of emanation, the pursuit of power in the service of incoherence, and still others may choose to enter into ways of deformation. However, it is not possible to create a new body politic or society without our neighbors and the members of our families. This reality demands the next step in our process: creating strategies of transformation. To enact as individuals and in groups new concrete manifestations of our eight archetypal relationships and archetypal dramas enacted in the way of life of transformation is to create a new politics and a new history. Enacting new relationships and stories of our lives as more loving and just faces of our underlying sources is the meaning of justice relevant for our times. It means to enact ways of relating and living and being that were not there before. This is our new-won freedom in act III, scenes 1 and 2, not only to choose among existing archetypal dramas but to create new ones that will do justice to ourselves, others, and to the source of sources.

This kind of participation is utterly democratic because it is available to each person. This theory is committed to awakening in each of us the capacity we have to tell a new story with personal, political, historical, and sacred implications. For this reason we need guides who witness to the process and awaken it in each of us. When any one of us enacts a transformation, we have made a personal breakthrough and created a new kind of politics by changing our environment for the better. For example, by building and staffing neighborhood centers that serve the young, the sick, the unemployed, and the elderly—that is, changed the parameters of what we can and need to do together—we have also opened a new historical path, inspired by a new and loving lord, by breaking inherited patterns that condemned people to docility and silence and replaced them with new and better ways of relating to each other that enabled the community to participate in the decisions that affect their lives.

Only in the service of transformation are the unconscious, conscious, creativity, linking with others, and justice kept in lively tension with the changing realities of life, for in the way of life of transformation, the concrete realization of transformation is never experienced as a final solution. To enter into the relationship of transformation becomes the final moment of a particular turn on the spiral process of transformation. The next turn will inevitably reveal new suffering and threats and new joys and opportunities, moving us down or up on this spiral. To live in the service of transformation is therefore persistently to experience an archetypal process of breaking relationships, moving into incoherence, and entering into the relationship of transformation anew. Through this same process, chains of emanations are turned into links of transformation.[22]

Unlike the arrested ways of life of emanation, incoherence, and deformation, the way of life of transformation frees us from our shyness, our fear of being naive or hurt, and empowers us to step forward militantly, yet nonviolently, with urgency and energy to protect and enhance our humanity and that of others. Since each of us is sacred as a face of the transforming god, our politics allows us to care and love others as we love and care for ourselves.

Authentic self-love allows us to love others as ourselves. The politics of blind loyalty in the service of emanation arrested in act I, scene 1 of the core drama, the rapacious enterpreneurship in the arrested way of life of incoherence in act II, scene 1, and the permanent crippling of others by entering the abyss as a result of exiting the core drama are consciously rejected and substituted with the love and commitment of act III, scenes 1 and 2 to include all others, to practice compassion and organize aggressively to empower all of us to redirect the use of our society's resources. This means to enact new forms of all eight archetypal relationships in the service of transformation, to participate in uprooting the inherited and destructive archetypal dramas/stories of our lives.

This freeing of ourselves of destructive social and political dramas allows us to initiate a new history wherein for the first time people are empowered together to form unions, task forces, rent strikes, co-ops, political parties, and immediately accessible affinity groups who nurture and care for the sick, old, and dying such as the recent creation of caring communities among gays to defy the isolation and powerlessness of those suffering from AIDS.[23] History takes now an upward turn on the spiral of life.

Our guide throughout this way of transforming life is not a master or tyrant who commands but a sacred source who invites and calls us to be participants on a common journey that will result in transforming the personal, political, historical, and sacred faces of our lives. To be aggressive, to step forward urgently in this way of life allows us to end the repression, suppression, and murder of self and other both psychically and physically; transforming of self, other, the world, and the sacred takes decisive and courageous steps in the service of love and compassion.

It is a great blessing that we can discern between the ways and stories of life and destruction; we are not predetermined to remain locked into a strategy of power or death. Yet, to choose strategies of aggressive response in the service of transformation will require a constant choice and willingness to enact a transforming solution to each particular problem. The three ways of emanation, incoherence, and deformation, because of their anesthetizing of the self, turn us into wounded and partial selves; in contrast, the persistent call to take the journey of transformation in regard to new problems is a witness to the indispensability of our loving and personal participation as whole persons. Without us as gods of transformation, the source of all sources will not be able to have a more just, loving, concrete, and sensual face.

Throughout the chapters that follow, we will give numerous examples from the stories and strategies of Latino families from the perspective of the theory of transformation. Any good theory must help us to see and understand what we have been living but which we have not fully understood. To reenvision our lives through a theory of transformation based on reflection and action exposes the threat of our present situation as well as the promise if we choose to live what most of us have intuitively known in our deepest depths.

NOTES

1. Manfred Halpern is at present writing his own manuscript, "Transformation: Its Theory and Practice in Personal, Political, Historical and Sacred Being." I have gained greatly from having read the various chapters of his manuscript in the writing of my own book.
2. Ibid.
3. Manfred Halpern, "Why Are Most of Us Partial Selves? Why Do

Partial Selves Enter the Road into Deformation?" A paper delivered at the 1991 Annual Meeting of the American Political Science Association, Washington, D.C.

4. Ibid.

5. Halpern, "Transformation."

6. For a further elaboration of the sacred, see David T. Abalos: *Latinos in the United States: The Sacred and the Political* (Notre Dame, Ind.: University of Notre Dame Press, 1986), and "Rediscovering the Sacred Among Latinos: A Critique from the Perspective of a Theory of Transformation," *The Latino Studies Journal*, 3, no. 2 (May 1992).

7. Iris M. Young, *Justice and the Politics of Difference* (Princeton, N.J.: Princeton University Press, 1990), pp. 39–65.

8. Stewart Robb, *Parsifal Libretto*, English version (New York: G. Schirmer, n.d.).

9. Manfred Halpern, "Notes on the Theory and Practice of Transformation," unpublished manuscript, Princeton University, 1980, p. 5.

10. Much of the summary above and the quotes from Halpern's theory are taken from Manfred Halpern's chapter, "Four Contrasting Repertories of Human Relations in Islam: Two Pre-Modern and Two Modern Ways of Dealing with Continuity and Change, Collaboration and Conflict and Achieving Justice," in *Psychological Dimensions of Near Eastern Studies*, ed. L. Carl Brown and Norman Itzkowitz. (Princeton, N.J.: The Darwin Press, 1977), p. 62; and from Chapter 7, "Archetypal Relationships," in Halpern, "Transformations."

11. Halpern, "Four Contrasting Repertories," p. 64.

12. Ibid.

13. Halpern, "Archetypal Relationships," pp. 9–10.

14. Ibid., p. 12.

15. Halpern, "Four Contrasting Repertories," pp. 77–78.

16. Halpern, "Archetypal Relationships," pp. 13–14.

17. Halpern, "Notes," p. 1.

18. Halpern, "Four Contrasting Repertories," pp. 78–79.

19. Halpern, "Archetypal Relationships," p. 18.

20. Halpern, "Notes," p. 1.

21. Ibid., p. 10.

22. Ibid.

23. In regard to creating a caring community for those suffering from AIDS, see Philip M. Kayal, *Bearing Witness: Gay Men's Health Crisis and the Politics of AIDS* (San Francisco: Westview Press, 1993). This book is written from the perspective of the theory of transformation.

Chapter Two

The Politics of *La Familia Latina*

POLITICS: A REDEFINITION

Political impotence is an often-cited criticism of the Latino community. In this chapter, traditional definitions of politics, which tend to focus on power or actions only within the public realm, are rejected, and politics is defined as relations and actions that shape our daily lives and environment in both personal and public realms. Relationships of domination and dependence that are characteristics of the patriarchal family must be challenged and broken before a politics of transformation can be practiced and in order to redefine politics as what we can and need to do together to create a family matrix that will prepare Latino youth for political participation in the public realm. Home and family life always prepares us to be political but in fundamentally different ways. Our choice must be that of participatory democracy in the service of transformation. "Politics is what we can and need to do together. Only when we turn our backs on conscious, critical and creative participation does politics become a realism dominated by power and powerlessness, violence and utopia."[1]

The view of politics being employed in this chapter is radically different from that of traditional political science. Politics here is being redefined to be what we can and need to do together; politics is a participatory experience to be practiced on a plane of equality with others by which we shape our daily lives and environment. To be political is also one of the four aspects of our very being. Thus we are always by the nature of our humanity enacting the personal, political, historical, and sacred faces of our being in all activities of our lives.

This conception and practice of politics rejects the views of such notable political experts as Hobbes, who saw politics as the pursuit of power after power; Machiavelli, who saw politics as the practice of gaining and maintaining power; Aristotle, for whom politics was the act of governing for white males (thus officially excluding most of the human race, which consisted and continues to consist of women, children, and people of color). These and other political philosophers have encouraged many to see the realm of politics as belonging only to that select group of legitimate, official people who somehow understand better than those for whom they made decisions the complex workings of society, the economy, and the body politic.[2]

My intent, therefore, is to present a view that seeks to restore politics to each of us as human beings, so that we can participate in the process of fostering families that nourish the best of what we have established, but also to recognize that ordinary people have the political authority to uproot or deinstitutionalize in order to create more responsive and just relationships.

This is a radically democratic proposition, because it dramatically expands the capacity of common people to shape political reality. This view of politics recognizes that we have the opportunity, by virtue of being human, to participate in the process of dissolving, creating, and nourishing institutions. In the final analysis, institutions are networks of human relationships that constitute all of us and that give us the freedom to participate. From this perspective, the family is the most critically important institution in one's preparation for political participation.

The political transformation of the family is what is really at stake. As was noted in Chapter One, transformation is the creation of fundamentally more loving and just relationships. Policy analysis as it is practiced at present in our country in relationship to the family is not interested in the politics of transformation. The liberal agenda of policy analysis is dominated by two questions: "What will benefit us, not them?" and "How can we get away with it?" These questions are asked in order to maintain the stability of the present system of politics. The greatest fear is anarchy, the breakdown of shared values, authority patterns, and political legitimacy.

Policy analysis never asks, "Why do we have this problem?" Policy analysts and practitioners, since they do their analysis in the logic of the way of life of incoherence, which is arrested in act II, do not ask ultimate questions because they accept society as it is. Therefore, they are unprepared to raise fundamental questions beyond existing political models about the pressing human dilemmas of our times: inequality, poverty, poor housing, child and spouse abuse, schooling, and nutrition, among others. To restore and maintain faith in the system—that is, to stabilize the situation—is their main concern.

As a result we no longer speak of real human beings who are the victims of economic dislocation or unemployment; they are turned into abstractions in mathematical models used to play out various scenarios. During mean and lean times for the less fortunate, such as the Reagan/Bush years, stability takes on a distorted face by pushing people to discover the furthest limits before the system is considered to be in trouble. For example, from 1977 to 1989, the top 1 percent of families took home 13 percent of all family income in the United States; while the bottom 40 percent of families suffered an actual decline in income.[3] In 1979 only 94,000 people reported an income of $200,000 or more to the IRS; ten years later this group rose to 790,000. Those reporting more than $1 million in income experienced a phenomenal increase from 3,601 in 1979 to 61,987 in 1989.[4]

To put this in perspective in relationship to the Latino community, the poverty rate of Latino families with children aged six to seventeen as of 1989 was 35.2 percent compared to 13.5 percent for European-American families.[5] This leads to the realization that the system was never meant to help the needy and that the much-vaunted safety net has failed, even though its primary purpose was always intended to cushion and protect the system. Where there is a problem with the system, whole armies of trained bureaucrats create a policy based on distributive justice, a justice that maintains the power structures of society because the dominant preserve the mechanism of decision-making in their own hands. Benefits are distributed as a form of direct bargaining in return for political loyalty enacted through the relationship of emanation.

This is really hierarchical politics and social engineering, a conscious attempt to depoliticize the vast majority of the people whose pain is buffered by appealing to their patriotism. Not surprisingly, therefore, the hurting members of society are so taken by the drama of incoherence that they cannot trace the causes of their pain to the way society is set up. This is a further witness to the power of the archetypal stories/dramas of our life to dominate us: we live them, we become them, and they take us over.

Policy analysis has a further problem. Our "best and brightest," as described by David Halberstam, are not immune from practicing profoundly immoral politics.[6] People like McGeorge Bundy and Robert McNamara were deeply disturbed by what the Vietnam War was doing to the social, economic, and political fabric of our country. They saw the threat to the nation; but in their discussions they did not anguish over the maimed bodies of both U.S. and Vietnamese victims of the bombings and systematic poisoning of the land with Agent Orange. For them the bottom line was a calculated and rational conclusion dictated by cost/benefit analysis. In the end we could not have guns and butter; the cost of war was too high, not in human lives, but rather in the effects on the economy, which would have negative political ramifications for them and their party. This clearly demonstrates the moral bankruptcy of the way of life of incoherence. Persons arrested in act II of the core drama are not capable, given the possessive power of this archetypal way of life, to see human beings as sacred but only as statistics to be counted and collected.[7]

THE POLITICS OF *LA FAMILIA LATINA* AND THE FOUR WAYS OF LIFE

Each of the four ways of life of emanation, incoherence, deformation, and transformation determines the ultimate meaning of our archetypal stories and relationships and frames the kind of politics we practice. Although these four ultimate ways of life have been described in detail in Chapter One, I will introduce each briefly within the context of the chapter.

Latinos enact the politics of the family in the four ultimate ways

of life, each of which is in the service of a particular god. The
archetypal way of life of emanation commands us from the depths
legitimized by a god of possessive jealousy demanding loyalty. This
sacred source is the god of emanation that inspires us and arrests
us in act I, scene 1 of the core drama.

The politics of the family in the service of this god and the way
of life of emanation

holds us within containers in which all we can and need to do together is
already codified and ritualized, and declared to be no longer a problem
except for the skill and intensity with which we affirm, elaborate, deepen
or refine what we are already performing together. The way of life of
emanation is a way of life in which a moment of truth has become frozen,
distorted or corrupted.[8]

The family as a necessary institution was used to justify locking
persons into permanent relationships that gave the family security
but at a great cost: the individual selfhood of its members.

It is this kind of family and politics within the present dominant
Latino culture that is being challenged and undermined. Similarly,
this kind of once-and-for-all truth enacted within the way of life
of emanation is dying everywhere. As we have seen in Chapter One,
the way of life of emanation has become so fragile because it is
increasingly unable to deal with the new consciousness and creativity that is especially evident in the lives and work of Latina
women.

When Latino families endowed with powerful emanational fragments begin to break down, it means that all of our concrete,
inherited relationships exercised within the family no longer give
us the capacity to deal with our lives. Thus when families from
Mexico, Puerto Rico, or El Salvador come to the United States,
they begin to learn and enact alternative patterns of behavior exercised in U.S. society. But even before coming here, Latino families
were affected by the shift from rural to urban centers with all of
the demands of the market society. That market society meant they
could no longer share common values in the service of emanation
that held the previous peasant society together. Adjusting to the
urban centers and to U.S. society really meant rejecting the old god
and allegedly becoming secular.[9]

But this was no mere secularization. In reality it meant the presence of a new but unrecognized sacred source because the city did
not accept the old gods. The new way of life, and its sacred source,
is the god of incoherence with a corresponding experience of fragmentation. The breaking and dying of the way of life of emanation
led many in the Latino family structure to choose the pursuit of
power as the new god within the service of incoherence, which, we
have seen, is to be permanently arrested in act II, scene 1 of the
core drama of transformation.

Politics as conventionally conceived—politics solely as the exercise of power—is the politics of preserving, enlarging, masking,
repressing, and profiting from incoherence. Politics in the service
of incoherence takes account of the fact that in the modern age, all
our concrete inherited forms of relationships are breaking, but
rather than facilitate change, fortresses that cannot be overcome
are built in deserts. For Latinos in the United States, survival has
meant building these impenetrable fortresses. In this society the
inherited authority of the father legitimized by the way of life of
emanation and concretely enforced through the relationships of
dependency—emanation, subjection, buffering, and direct exchange—began to crumble.

As members of the family began to adopt new relationships, such
as boundary management, direct exchanges and isolation in the
service of incoherence, it caused an incoherence in the family. This
experience of incoherence was often met by resorting to the use of
the relationship of subjection as naked force. However in this case
the relationship of subjection is no longer used to maintain the
emanational way of life but is now enacted in the service of deformation. Thus deformation is practiced as a way of life because it
allows the illusion of male supremacy to be perpetuated even though
it has lost its legitimacy.

Male domination has become an illusion precisely because the
cultural, social, and political structures as well as the way of life
of emanation and the limited repertory of the eight relationships
that upheld and justified this inherited story of patriarchy are no
longer accepted as legitimate by an increasing number of Latinos.
Those who respond in order to force others back to an alleged
normalcy exit the core drama and enter into a politics of violence
and revenge that makes life fundamentally worse.

A fourth possibility for the Latino family is politics practiced in the way of life of transformation in act III, scenes 1 and 2 of the core drama of transformation. The sacred source and way of life in this context demand that we continuously persist in creating and nourishing fundamentally new and better relationships. In the way of life of transformation, all eight of the archetypal relationships are available to shape the daily encounters of life. There is no longer a limited repertory of relationships. All are now free to enact relationships that allow them the capacity to confront ever-emerging problems. For example, in the service of transformation the relationship of emanation, which had been used to permanently link loyal subjects to mysterious rulers and children to godlike parents, is now enacted as a temporary relationship to allow children and adults to draw love and affirmation from others so they can return to their lives.

As was stated in Chapter One, the eight archetypal relationships are neither negative nor creative in themselves; they draw their ultimate meaning and purpose from the way of life in which they are enacted. In the way of life of transformation we become conscious of within which act and scene we were caught in the core drama, which story we were living, the relationships that were being practiced, and the way of life that gave life its underlying meaning. This awareness of the choices available empowers us to affirm that it is our inalienable right to demand that relations between men and women, parents and children, the individual person and the outward realization of her or his inner dreams be recognized as issues of political justice that make it imperative to find new and better connections with each other.[10]

All aspects of male/female relationships and all relationships within the family are therefore political. If the family environment— that is, the existing story, the way of life, the relationships that link the members of the family together—do not allow each individual to grow to full potential, then we have a political problem. In the final analysis, only our authentic selves, not selves that have been imposed upon us, are capable of creating history, rather than being victims of a corrupted past.

THE LATINO FAMILY: ARRESTED IN THE SERVICE OF EMANATION

None of us is an individualist as our liberal society would have us believe. All of us have been born and reared into a web of relationships. We are the products and handiwork of our parents, our culture and history, our relationships to significant others, and to our unconscious, sacred sources. To discover, recognize, and name this network of relationships and stories in our own personal and collective history is to discover both the connecting and disconnecting patterns of our lives. If we fail to do this we will waste our time beating the air and attacking phantoms.

Latino history and culture in general has not been kind to Latinos when they look for help to guide them in regard to creating a new kind of family and male/female relationships. Indeed, their ancestors lived for the most part in the way of life of emanation of fixed faith and frozen patterns of behavior. This kind of family politics prepared their foremothers and forefathers to accept the hierarchical social arrangements that prevailed in the Spanish state of Los Reyes Catolicos, the Jewish synagogue, and, finally, in the various indigenous empires of the new world. This hierarchy was capped and legitimized by males both divine and human.

At the heart of the family is the relationship between men and women. Both European and indigenous cultures institutionalized the inferiority of women. Our Native American ancestors, for example, valued women for their loyalty in upholding the real purpose for their existence: giving birth to future warriors, taking care of the needs of men and children, and providing pleasure. Two very important Aztec goddesses took their names from these functions: Cihuateteo was the name given to women who died in the battle of giving birth; prostitutes, women who provided pleasure, were named Ahuianime and were protected by the goddess of pleasure, Tlazolteotl. The Spaniards also used a double standard: the woman who took care of them and procreated their children did not have to be the same women who gave pleasure. Thus *la casa chica*, the second household for a man's lover, was institutionalized and blessed by our history and culture several centuries ago.[11]

The Catholic Church frowned on the institutionalization of the mistress but as long as the church was unwilling to tackle its own view of women as inferior, it was in no position to be taken seriously. As a result, the church took an approach toward women that mirrored its preaching regarding the treatment of the Indians and the peons. In both cases the church acted as a mediator to lighten the burden of women and peons, but without questioning the system itself. In this way the church actually helped to strengthen the inferior status of both women and campesinos, permanently retarded as children in the way of life of emanation. The role of the church was to help people accept and live with the system by reforming its harshness from time to time. This actually became a god's will, but again, the will of the god of emanation in act I, scene 1, wherein all truth was finished and all people could do was accept it.

The resulting subjection of Latina women in this way has made them perpetual mothers because their only fulfillment has come from exercising influence over their children, who in turn they often do not allow to grow up. Latina mothers do not consciously and coldly wound their children in this way. This is not their personal, subjective ego speaking, but rather the power of an underlying sacred source, the archetypal drama of patriarchy that draws its strength from the god of emanation. This archetypal story of the inherited Latino past saw to it that Latina mothers were lamed, possessing their children to cover their own lack of love and passion with their husbands.

Mothers living within the story of patriarchy have often said to their male offspring, "No se te vaya olvidar quien viene primero en tu vida" (Don't you ever forget who comes first in your life), in front of the son's wife. Ironically, in choosing his wife, the Latino man has already sought a maternal figure, usually not even aware of this underlying archetypal drama.[12] Thus Latinas and Latinos were doomed to repeat the past because there was no self present to challenge the political domination of the patriarchs who repeated history as the will of god.

The politics of sexism inherent in the story of patriarchy destroys both the man and the woman, the wife and husband, and wounds the next generation. Intimacy and passion are possible only between equals. A man who sees a wife as a shadow of his mother cannot relate to her as an equal because she is either above him, on a pedestal, or because she fails to meet up to the expectations of being like his mother, she is below him. Other women are not burdened by such associations and can become a source of sexual release. Yet here again there is no fulfillment because while she might be a good woman, conventional values tell us that she is still a woman of ill repute and therefore inferior.

The Latino male living within and perpetuating the dying way of life of emanation is thus a victim of his own heritage. He knows that it is the woman who provides continuity, who raises the children in the face of abandonment, and creates the emotional environment. Yet he harbors ambivalent feelings toward women, a mixture of loyalty and honor with distrust and anxiety. Each generation of Latinos, men and women alike, has inherited the grave consequences of this story.

This is a perspective that sees Latino culture as contradictory, as both creative and destructive. These relationships make sense given a whole way of life stunted in act I, scene 1 that has necessarily emphasized survival in the throes of hostility by emphasizing family continuity, cooperation, and security, and which has thus discouraged the individual, especially women, from initiating change and conflict. However, a great price has been paid for unquestioning loyalty to this way of life: the fulfillment of the core drama of transformation is rendered impossible and with it one's experiences, dreams, hopes, and feelings have been denied.

If Latinos are to avoid romanticizing their cultural past, they must painfully but truthfully seek to heal it by going beyond overly protective attitudes on the one hand, and destructive criticism on the other. They must be willing to polarize with the culture, to enter into act II, scene 1, wherein they break with the emanational force of the culture, to rebel against it and thereby to shatter its mystique. A community cannot continue to believe blindly in the way of life of emanation. But neither should it choose the way of incoherence as the successful model for Latinos.

ASSIMILATION INTO THE WAY OF LIFE OF INCOHERENCE

The Latino family entered into a whole new way of life, that of incoherence, when the families were displaced from the land and forced to migrate to the cities or the United States. The displacement was due to many factors: revolution, drought, economic policy of the central government, economic imperialism, foreign subversion of legitimate revolutions, or, in a money society, inability to raise enough currency to live. The move from rural to urban life shattered the web of life of emanation that people had come to accept as given by god. In the cities they met their fellow *paisanos* but it was different; they were not the same as country people. City people were wise in a different way—*listos* (eager and willing)—they had learned new patterns of behavior, especially the relationship of boundary management and, in addition, had accepted the whole new way of life of incoherence, the pursuit of power, as the life of the city. The god and way of life of emanation were of little value in this new pursuit, but because they felt guilty leaving the entire way of emanation behind they still went to the church and recited the inherited prayers.

But this was now the peripheral part of their life; these prayers and ceremonies still constituted powerful but nevertheless mere fragments of this dying way of life. The way of life of incoherence offered no ultimate "why" or meaning to people's lives except the pursuit of self-interest and power. This explanation, I believe, helps to explain why Oscar Lewis's families experienced such traumatic changes in the urban center.[13] Women often took power because the males were not able to adjust to the new demands. The men's inability to respond meant they could not dominate or bargain or provide the security of the relationship of emanation. Women learned new relationships, primarily the previously forbidden relationship of boundary management, with which to compete in the larger society.

Men still knew how to manipulate the guilt of women by appealing to fragments of the dying way of life of emanation. These two competing ways of life, of emanation and incoherence, provided further confusion in the lives of parents and children in the family. The children saw the change in the patterns, the loss of authority and respect. This breaking led to their rejection of the inherited and limited repertory of relationships that they now considered to be powerless in this society. The father, who was conscious of his loss of power and respect, frequently turned to violence to reassert control and thus entered into deformation.

For a time, force and appeals to guilt, sin, and shame created a safe haven for males in their own home as an assertion of the way of life of emanation, while in the public realm the larger society forced all into new patterns in the service of incoherence. These new patterns were those of asserting one's own autonomous personality based on new skills that were marketable. In addition, to

make money, the husband/father had to agree to give women time
away from home, the relationship of isolation. The ability to learn
and earn for women gave them increased bargaining power. If the
father became impossible, the mother could now evict him from
the home; women now experienced some domination over men. In
many cases, inherited roles were reversed. But this kind of change
did not transform; it merely altered the terms of power in a reformation and substituted women for men as the dominators while
leaving the old system of inherited power relationships intact.

Because of this heritage, many Latinas have rejected the structures
of the Latino family enacted in the service of emanation. In this
country, Latina women can make comparisons to the relative freedom of other women. As a result many have chosen to marry outside
the culture in order to escape the dominating Latino male. Often
this has been a form of assimilation for Latinas who believed that
other cultures have better male/female relations. But the dominant
culture in the service of incoherence offers rational marriages, based
on mutual rights, obligations, and contracts.[14] Its rhetoric is that
marriage is for love, but in reality it is firmly founded on a bedrock
of power. It is true that women have less power in comparison to
men in U.S. society, but they can gain power through achieving
new skills for which opportunities are available.

The access to birth control, economic freedom, the feminist movement, and a society committed to equal opportunity have had a
powerful impact on the Latino family structure in the United States.
Yet the old way of life of emanation remains side by side with the
new assimilated way of life of incoherence. As a result many Latinos
live conflicted lives, using different patterns and vacillating between
the ways of life of emanation and incoherence, caught between acts
I and II of the core drama. Others have bitterly renounced the old
culture and family reared in the way of emanation and have identified it with stigma.

CHOOSING BETWEEN WAYS OF LIFE AND DEATH

Deformation is the choice to create fundamentally new but also
fundamentally worse relationships. Deformation is any act that
diminishes our humanity. As the traditional Latino family living
within the way of emanation breaks, the resulting experience of

incoherence can lead people to sheer violence in an attempt to restore the old *respeto* (respect) and authority. In their efforts to return to the dying way of life of emanation, they have to deny the reality of the individual who is breaking away. The authority of the·father, for example, is considered sacred and so masculine authority, which is a fragment of the way of life of emanation, is endowed with a pseudo sacred legitimacy.

In reality this is no longer the way of emanation but a false way of life of emanation because it is based on a lie: male supremacy. The relationship of incoherence, due to the breaking of emanation, is now experienced: two people stand in the presence of each other and cannot agree on how to relate. In regard to the core drama this is act II, scene 1, wherein we break with the person with whom we were previously linked in emanation in act I. Because the breaking of connections has not been acceptable to the rejected authority figure, usually the father or husband, the incoherence often leads to violence and so we end with a qualitatively worse way of deformation. Because the women in the family no longer accept the legitimacy of male dominance, they feel violated by such an effort to restore it. There is no security, a characteristic of emanation, and there is also no longer an unconscious surrender of the self. To try to push people back to a state of unconsciousness is not possible. The psychic and physical violence employed thus no longer occurs in the name of emanation but becomes deformation.

THE WAY OF LIFE OF TRANSFORMATION

There is a fourth choice, a fourth way of life available to us, that of transformation. This way of life demands a fourfold process: the transformation of oneself, one's neighbor, the world, and the sacred. For the first time individuals can step forward as persons, free to create conflict and change; to experience new consciousness, creativity, and new linkages to others. Each person counts and all are impoverished if anyone violates us and prevents our coming forth in all of the acts of the core drama of transformation. We have the opportunity to be a participatory self wherever we find ourselves. All aspects of our lives are available to us to be shaped by our choices.

But in order to fulfill the core drama of transformation as explained in Chapter One, one must go beyond the rebellion of act II, scene 1 and enter into act II, scene 2, where not only the actual men who dominated are rejected, but also the archetypal story of patriarchy that gave men their mysterious hold over Latinas and the way of life of emanation in which the Latino community lived this story. Emanation as a way of life as well as the ways of life of incoherence and deformation need to be rejected or they will end up crippling the life of the Latino family over and over again.

CREATING THE ALTERNATIVE: THE FAMILY AS TRANSFORMING RELATIONSHIPS IN MOTION

The family remains a necessary institution for all of us. It provides us with the necessary security, affection, and continuity to begin the process of individuation. The family can serve as a merciful container wherein its members can become mutual guides to each other through the various acts and scenes of the core drama as they live the stories of their lives.

But often Latinos failed to see that patterns of relationship emphasizing security and protection were only temporary. In the hostile area in which most Latinos grew up it was essential to have a close-knit protective family. This has led too many Latinos in this country to romanticize and to pass over abuses in the family. Latinos must be careful that in their resistance against the critique of their culture they do not glibly state that everything Latino is good. Revolutions have to remain consciously critical of self and other and not allow a tribal fusion as a new form of emanation to hide the problems. We require courage based on a new consciousness to grow our own marriages and families, which are neither Anglo-Saxon nor blindly Latino.

There is no attempt here to consider love, affection, emotion, or close relationships as outmoded. A family that as a group is dedicated to the liberation of its individual members will never be out of date. We need the family but in a qualitatively different way. Too often love is oppressive. Love in the way of life of emanation means uncritical loyalty and acceptance of the loved one; love in the service of transformation entails mutuality and equality wherein both males and females discover each other as friends and lovers.

This means that Latinas and Latinos as friends and lovers have successfully emptied themselves of the drama of patriarchy and experienced wholeness in regard to at least this one aspect of their lives. Since they have experienced the core drama of transformation they can become guides in act III, scene 2 as parents escorting their children through the core drama of transformation.

Love in the service of transformation involves being able to create conflict and change as well as continuity and cooperation so that all members of the family may grow their own personhood. What we need is love that frees us to have what no one can command: the decision to shape our own selfhood. This is the inner, sacred force that begins to insist that the family give us space both internal and external. Thus to perpetuate relationships beyond the time that they are necessary and to fail to transform our linkages is to create neurotic personalities.

Giving birth to and nourishing the next generation is sacred and political work. Latino family politics practiced in the way of life of transformation can allow the nurturing of each child to emerge as a full self. This kind of socialization can prepare children for a particular kind of task: radical participation in shaping their daily lives wherever they find themselves. Politics is what we can and need to do together; furthermore, politics is participation with others by which we shape our daily lives and world.

Family life, therefore, is always political; either we prepare children for a life of being dominated and possessed in order, in their turn, to control and possess others, or we guide them to transformation. To question, to criticize, to dissent in the family context prepares our children to question all authority. Rearing children with a fear of punishment and appeals to authority, and not allowing them to create conflict and change, prepares them for authoritarian liberalism wherein they can pursue their own self-interest and power as long as they are loyal to the powerful in the service of emanation. Contract marriages and families that stress power, individual autonomy, and individualism prepare children to compete with others in the larger society of liberal democracy in the way of life of incoherence.

The stories of possessive love and patriarchy, as pseudo emanations that give a phony mystique to the fragment of masculinity, legitimize violence and the inferior status of women so that deformation destroys any possibility of men and women creating equally fulfilling relationships. Any society that wounds half of its people is certainly preparing its members not for democratic participation but for dictatorship. On the other hand, to live in a family where each person is treated with respect as a person in the way of life of transformation is a beginning for true democratic citizenship where each appreciates both self and others as sacred.[15]

Children are always learning and being prepared to reproduce, in their relationships outside the family, the kind of politics and community they have experienced in the home. These different kinds of politics, as we have seen, are enacted in four different ways of life. Each of these four ultimate choices will mean a different kind of democratic politics: elitist democracy, practiced within a small elite but not in the society at large, as in the way of life of emanation; liberal democracy, which legitimizes unequal access to power, as in the way of incoherence; democratic nationalism, which shapes another form of blind loyalty intended to punish the outsiders, as in the way of life of deformation; or participatory democracy, which encourages the fulfillment of each of its citizens, as in the service of transformation.

All are called "democracy," but we now realize, given our understanding of the deep life opened up by the knowledge of archetypal ways of life, that we can go beyond labels to grasp the underlying reality behind the word. There are four fundamentally different archetypal ways of life underlying the same term. Our challenge as Latinas and Latinos is to guide our children to create a fundamentally new and loving democratic society in both our families and in the public realm in the service of transformation.

NOTES

1. Manfred Halpern, "Choosing Between Ways of Life and Death and Between Forms of Democracy: An Archetypal Analysis," *Alternatives: A Journal of World Politics*, Winter 1986–87, p. 6. (Published by the Center for the Study of Developing Societies, Delhi, India, and the Institute for World Order, New York.)

2. In writing this chapter, I was deeply influenced by Manfred Halpern's paper cited above. It is a brilliant analysis of the archetypal drama of democracy, which inspired my understanding of the Latino family choosing between four archetypal ways of life.

3. Sylvia Nasar, "The 1980's: A Very Good Time for the Very Rich," *New York Times*, March 2, 1992, p. 1.

4. As reported in the *New York Times*, December 1, 1991.

5. Luis Dunay and Karen Pittman, *Latino Youths at a Crossroads*, an Adolescent Pregnancy Prevention Clearinghouse report by the Children's Defense Fund, January–March 1990. (CDF Publications, 122 C Street N.W., Washington, D.C. 20001.)

6. See David Halberstam, *The Best and the Brightest* (New York: Random House, 1972).

7. Manfred Halpern, "Radically Different Faces of the Sacred," Chapter 8 in "Transformation: Its Theory and Practice in Personal, Political, Historical and Sacred Being" (unpublished manuscript). In addition see David T. Abalos, "Transformative Commitment: A New Paradigm for the Study of the Religious, *Journal of Dharma*, 6, no. 3 (July–September 1981).

8. Manfred Halpern, "Notes on the Theory and Practice of Transformation," an unpublished manuscript, Princeton University, 1980, p. 1. See also his "Choosing Between Ways of Life and Death," pp. 8–9 and 13–24.

9. For an excellent portrayal of how the journey from the rural centers helped to destroy a whole way of life, I know of no better reading than Rene Marques, *La Carreta* (Rio Piedras, P.R.: Editorial Cultural, 1971).

10. Ibid., pp. 1–2. See also Halpern, "Choosing Between Ways of Life and Death," pp. 43–54.

11. Alan Riding, *Distant Neighbors: A Portrait of the Mexicans* (New York: Alfred A. Knopf, 1985), is one of the best books that has been written by an American about Mexican history and culture.

12. See Chapter 3, "The Politics of the Latino Family," in David T. Abalos, *Latinos in the United States: The Sacred and the Political* (Notre Dame, Ind.: University of Notre Dame Press, 1986).

13. Oscar Lewis, *Five Families* (New York: New American Library, 1959).

14. For a good discussion of the rational marriage, see Ann Belford Ulanov, *The Feminine* (Evanston, Ill.: Northwestern University Press, 1972).

15. For a parallel view of how teachers prepare the young for sacred and political participation, see David T. Abalos, "The Teacher as Guide," *Journal of Dharma*, 11, no. 1 (January–March 1986), pp. 62–75.

Chapter Three

Tracing the Inherited Stories
of the Latino Family

The material that follows is based on a series of interviews, discussions, and personal observations. For the sake of preserving the privacy of the individuals and families involved, I have decided to present the empirical evidence in a composite manner—that is, merging together people from different families and from various parts of the country. Furthermore, I have changed the names of those interviewed, and changed the locales. All of this has been done in a way to preserve the authenticity of the experiences of the Latino family that we are analyzing from the perspective of the theory of transformation. Our theoretical approach allows us to trace inherited archetypal dramas and ways of life across several generations so that we can clearly see the effect of uncritically repeating the past and the urgency to create new dramas of the Latino family in the service of transformation.

THE FIRST GENERATION OF *LA FAMILIA LATINA* IN THE UNITED STATES: THE MARRIAGE AND FAMILY OF EMILIANO AND JOSEFA

For nearly four thousand years women have shaped their lives and acted under the umbrella of patriarchy, specifically a form of patriarchy best described as paternalistic dominance. The term describes the relationship of a dominant group, considered superior, to a subordinate group, considered inferior, in which the dominance is mitigated by mutual obligations and reciprocal rights. The dominated exchange submission for protection, unpaid labor for maintenance. In the patriarchal family, responsibilities and obligations are not equally distributed among those to be protected: the male children's subordination to the father's dominance is temporary; it lasts until they themselves become heads of households. The subordination of female children and of wives is lifelong. Daughters can escape it only if they place themselves as wives under the dominance/protection of another man. The basis of paternalism is an unwritten contract for exchange: economic support and protection given by the male for subordination in all matters, sexual service, and unpaid domestic service given by the female. Yet the relationship frequently continues in fact and in law, even when the male partner has defaulted on his obligation.[1]

Emiliano migrated to this country from his native Colombia in 1923. Three years later he sent for his young wife, Josefa, and their first child, Racquel. Neither Josefa nor Emiliano had any formal schooling; they could not read or write. Life was very difficult for them in Gary, Indiana, where Emiliano had come looking for work in the steel plants. Six more children were born in various cities in the Midwest. Just as the family was beginning to get on it's feet, Emiliano was hit by a virus and died at the age of forty. Josefa was left with seven children, $1,500 in savings, no marketable skills, no extended family, and no awareness as to how this country worked. As a result of the trauma of Emiliano's death, Josefa withdrew into herself and relied more and more on the older children to supervise their younger siblings and to do the general housework.

Josefa felt alone, inadequate, and hesitant in an Anglo, urban world. Without her husband Josefa was totally bereft. She was especially vulnerable because nothing in her background had prepared her to raise a family on her own in a strange country where she still could not speak English. Josefa had been raised to be totally dependent on men, especially when it came to the public, wider world. Josefa had certainly been a recipient of the benefits of her socialization into the story of patriarchy but now she realized the cost of feminine dependence.

So powerful was the patriarchal drama in her life that after fifty years, half a century, Josefa could not even bring herself to criticize her husband because it was being disloyal to his memory. The following are essential to the story of patriarchy: excessive deference to men, possessive love, male domination; male superiority over women often based on religious grounds; sexually, economically, intellectually, and politically subordinate women. Women, for their part, have for millenia participated in their own subordination because they have been psychologically prepared to accept their own inferiority.[2]

Josefa had not even been married a year when she felt betrayed by her husband. Josefa's mother-in-law controlled Emiliano, who felt especially devoted to his mother since his father was killed in a *venganza* (feud) in Colombia. Emiliano's mother felt threatened by Josefa as a competing source of emanation and so turned her son against his wife by lying about an act of arrogance on Josefa's part. Emiliano was constrained by the archetypal story of patriarchy to prove that he was the head of the household; and so he struck Josefa with a leather strap for her seeming impertinence.

From that day, Josefa admitted, but only after many years, that she no longer had the same affection for Emiliano. Emiliano had upheld his mother, his manhood, and inherited status as head of the family in the way of life of emanation but at a very great price. Josefa's mother-in-law felt vindicated because her son believed her and not his wife; Josefa knew, as the wives of her own sons would experience years later, that it was all over before it began. Either a wife submitted or she went crazy. There were not many options given the power of the story of patriarchy in the way of life of emanation. The lack of alternatives was not only due to economic causes; the most debilitating reason was to be found in the crippling presence of the archetypal drama of patriarchy.

Even if a woman was fortunate enough in those days to have a job, education, skills, and opportunities, she was immobilized not only by the actual husband, male guardian, or father, but by the story of patriarchy, enacted in the service of emanation arrested in act I, scene 1 that gave men their mysterious power over women. In the service of emanation women were limited to patterns of dependency, usually the relationships of emanation, subjection, isolation, buffering, and direct exchange. Their lives were dominated by the emphasis on continuity and cooperation with men as the source of their life with little or no ability to create conflict and change; the justice they experienced for their silence, even though it might be an angry silence, was security. However, this security had a heavy price: they could not live or express their own desires.

Years later in the United States, because of Emiliano's lack of affection, Josefa dedicated herself to the family and especially to her oldest son. Emiliano never allowed Josefa to question him about the most mundane issues, such as how much money he made, where he went after work, or who his friends were. Josefa felt that she had no right to know and even stated that she was not one of those women who interfered in her husband's affairs.

Over the years Josefa never forgave her mother-in-law; yet, ironically, she did not realize that she was raising her own sons just as her mother-in-law had reared her own husband, dominated by the story of patriarchy. Indeed, after Emiliano's death, Josefa became a female patriarch, or matriarch; she had merely reformed the drama to accommodate a change of gender. In the way of life of emanation it is disloyal to give your allegiance to another competing source of emanation. We are in the presence here once again of a sacred story that takes over our lives.

To know these dramas and how they work is to understand why when Josefa's second oldest son was married it was a traumatic experience for her. Josefa saw the wedding as an act of disloyalty. She was almost totally irrational the whole day. The sad irony is that Josefa had become her mother-in-law; Josefa had rejected her actual mother-in-law but because she had not emptied herself of the drama of patriarchy that had controlled her life on the deeper level, she repeated again in her own life, with her own son the disabling story of patriarchy in the service of emanation, arrested in act I, scene 1.

THE SECOND GENERATION: INHERITING THE STORY OF PATRIARCHY

Emiliano died when Luis, the youngest child, was four years old. Josefa was a distant figure who seldom gave him any affection, although she would accept it if offered. Luis perceived that his mother was strong at home but weak in the outside world. Ever since he could remember, his mother was sick and, therefore, could not take care of the children. His sisters became his mothers when they were very young. Out of sheer anger at their heavy responsibility, his sisters were often very physical in the treatment of him.

As a child Luis grew up surrounded by violence both psychological and physical. To be hit with a belt, a board, a fist, or to have his hair pulled was part of his everyday existence inside the home and in the neighborhood. Racial and ethnic taunts were commonplace. As the youngest in a family of seven he often bore the brunt of the resentment from his siblings because they had to take care of him. Even at school he received the strap or a ruler across the hand for fighting or breaking other rules. As an aspiring member of a gang, he had to beat up boys from rival gangs to prove himself to his peers. Luis saw relatives get hit and even witnessed the physical assault on his own mother by an irate male roomer in their home.

Luis became afraid of violence and really could not stand to see people get hurt. But he had to hide his fear because it was part and parcel of everyday life. Luis was experiencing the drama of tribalism, the story that tells people who come from communities of color that they are not valuable. As a result he was often physically challenged as a "Spic." His second oldest brother was small but very strong and so defended himself with his fists. The oldest brother was devastating with his tongue and could demolish people verbally. Luis began increasingly to survive by being a "sincere, sweet boy." In other words, he repressed his anger and hurt and dealt with violence through self-righteous projection. At this time in his young life he discovered religion and became antiviolence, antisex, antigang, and antiwhatever was not fitting for a good Catholic boy. Other people did these things but he was now above it all. In this way Luis could get away from being a "dirty Greaser" and become acceptable to the "better" people.

This repression of his anger would surface from time to time in irrational ways that surprised Luis, but he would always buffer it away by stating that that wasn't the real me. To avoid problems he developed into a loner. He worked every day in a local grocery store, did homework, paid bills, went to church services, and developed a reputation as a responsible and religious young man. The Irish Catholic women in the parish became his adopted mothers. But all the time he was too serious and did not really enjoy himself. So in addition to repressing his sexuality as an adolescent, Luis also failed to deal with his potential for violence and the perpetuation of a fear of his own rage. He could not deal with these issues in his young life because he was in full flight from his Latino background and himself.

After the death of Luis's father, the family's poverty was very stark. His mother was forced to take a job to pay the bills. Luis's brothers and sisters slept three or four to a bedroom. Over the years in these conditions the children saw a lot of fighting related to alcohol. Luis vividly remembers pouring whiskey down the drain while several people were fighting in the kitchen. One of his sisters at the age of ten took a man to court for terrorizing the family. Luis's baptismal godfather was a great influence on him at this early age. He drank heavily, fought a lot, and went out with a lot of women because his wife, who was Luis's godmother, was in Colombia.

Luis associated his godfather together with all of the other Latino men with whom he had such bad experiences. Luis reacted to his godfather's treatment of women by vowing that he would never be like Latino males who seemed to spend so much of their time carousing and drinking. Luis was desperate for guidance and protection. He felt betrayed by the adult males in the community whom he felt were the very cause of his fears. He saw them as the perpetrators of violence against his anchor, his mother, and all other women whom he identified with his mother. For all of these reasons Luis didn't want to be a "typical" Latino male—husband or father.

At this early part of his life Luis could not identify the drama of patriarchy within himself; he felt that if he could get away from the community, from the actual men, then he would be safe. In order to get away he was able to leave home with a scholarship and attended college in the Southwest. After graduating with an engineering degree, Luis met and married his wife, Carmen.

The story of patriarchy is the drama that Luis sensed but could not name or put his finger on. He knew that at the heart of the inherited Latino family there was something that devoured people. On this account, he was very hesitant to marry a Latina woman for fear that he would get caught up in forces that he feared but did not understand. But Luis had already inherited and internalized the drama of patriarchy. It didn't matter if Luis had married a Latina or an Anglo, it would not have prevented him from being a patriarchal male. Nor would assimilation, becoming a liberated Anglicized male in the way of life of incoherence, have made any real difference.

Logical, rational attempts to protect ourselves with contractual or ideological limits are completely incapable of dealing with the underlying dramas involved. As a result these limits build a false hope that patriarchy has been eradicated. Luis was powerless to do or be anything but a patriarchal, Latino male in act I, scene 1 until he rejected the drama of patriarchy in act II, scenes 1 and 2 and until he discovered his capacity to participate in creating more loving and just alternative archetypal dramas in the service of transformation in act III, scenes 1 and 2. Thus contract marriages and intellectual liberation become merely reform and rebellion. Rebellion strengthens the archetypal dramas because we fight the concrete, specific person and miss the underlying archetypal dramas that control our life.

In other aspects of Latino life, Luis's father, brothers, godfather, and sons enacted and are enacting other stories in this society—stories that are too often in the service of incoherence. Luis's father worked hard and long hours to feed and house the family. Nothing was below him when it came to providing for them; he sold apples, cut hair, and did day work. He joined a union, the AFL/CIO, when unions were not popular. Luis's father learned to maneuver his way through the urban system for them. Much of this activity was made possible because he had learned power relations—that is, the relationships of autonomy, direct exchange, and isolation in the service of incoherence to be able to protect the way of life of emanation in the family.

If Luis and others are to carry forth the best in their culture, it will not be choosing one value because it is Latino and another value from European-American society because it is needed to perform well in this system. We are not after a mixture here but the weaving of new archetypal dramas that will allow us to live them in a fundamentally new and better way within the consciousness of transformation. This means not hanging onto fragments of the dying way of life of emanation, such as uncritical acceptance of the Latino family so that we can have a safe haven to which to return from the daily battles waged in the service of incoherence.

Such a schizoid mixture would merely serve to perpetuate the worst in both cultures and societies because they balance each other. When there is change it is always manipulated to be system maintenance change. To reenvision everything from the perspective of transformation means to care deeply about others so that actual changes result to make life fundamentally more loving and compassionate. In this way we are free to create new manifestations of the previously forbidden relationships, such as boundary management. Boundary management is no longer enacted as an assimilated Anglo relationship in the service of incoherence, but as a means by which to achieve the necessary skills that give us the leverage to protect our humanity and that of all others in the service of transformation. In this way relationships do not remain artificially Latino or European-American but are rediscovered and re-created in the way of transformation. It is for this reason that the eight relationships are not negative or creative in themselves because they draw their deeper meaning and quality from the way of life in which they are enacted.

THE PATRIARCHAL MARRIAGE AND FAMILY OF LUIS AND CARMEN: RAISING THE THIRD GENERATION

In his marriage Luis could no longer repress the drama of patriarchy. He was not happy but did not know why. On occasion he could intuit his problems but, not having discovered the reality of archetypal stories, he actually did not know what he was facing. It was very difficult for him to admit that he was just like the Latino men from whom he had tried to get away. For too long Luis did not allow his children to grow up. It was partially an escape from having to form a more mature relationship to them. If you dedicate your life to your job, your "family" as an abstraction, or other pursuits, you can avoid facing real people. All archetypal dramas, except those lived in the service of transformation, have this effect because they preserve us as partial and wounded selves.

Because Luis repressed the inherited patriarchal drama, he remained arrested in act I, scene 1 of the core drama in relationship to this aspect of his life. In other dimensions of his life, Luis was very competent at his job and as a consultant for national engineering groups. But at home he often violently exploded in times of stress and incoherence. He would turn to joking and playfulness in order to hide its emergence against his will. This gave rise to a sense of guilt. When he was not taken seriously, he laughed but remained angry. The constant presence of anger was a clear indication that something was wrong. In the core drama this is what act I, scene 2 is all about. We receive hints, inspirations, feelings, dreams, ideas from our inner voice that awaken us to the reality underlying our lives.

Finally, Luis began to take responsibility for his anger and immaturity. This helped him to see how complex his life was, how each person is a bundle of connections, relating to different people with aspects of their being. For example, as an engineer, his colleagues would never have guessed such difficulties. In regard to his job, Luis is in total command and at ease. Thus it depends on what specific issue, what face of one's life, which characters are on stage, what drama is at stake and in which overarching way of life we enact our lives. Above all, what Luis has come to learn is that it makes all the difference in the world for us to be aware of the dramas that we are living together with others. Whether we want to or not we all bring our baggage—that is, our dramas and unfinished stories—into the lives of our families.

The real tragedy is that Luis's wife, Carmen, and his children began to "adjust" or live with the violence inherent in the drama of patriarchy. But because they were living in an environment permeated with patriarchy, their coping mechanisms prolonged the drama by making it more tolerable. Luis's inherited Latino patriarchal relationships in the service of emanation led him to repeat much of his painful past.

After graduating from college, Carmen got married with the hope that finally she would be able to get away from her dominating family to be loved as an individual and as an adult. When she realized that she was back where she started, in act I, scene 1 in her father's house, she saw it as a cruel awakening and then settled in for the long haul by repressing her inner voice in act I, scene 2 that warned her to get out of this marriage. The resulting repression frustrated her creativity, and she developed a sense of doubt in her own abilities. She tried over and over to make herself into a woman that she thought Luis would find attractive and worthy of his love and attention. In total desperation, Carmen made a conscious decision to withdraw and not to risk herself again with a person who was repeatedly unfaithful and immature. In order not to be vulnerable, Carmen had to violate crucial aspects of her own life.

This kind of mutilation present in both Luis and Carmen is in the service of deformation. Once again we can see the results of the fragility of the way of life of emanation. It is not possible for this way of life to respond to Carmen's needs. By turning herself into a partial self in order to persist in emanation, she must wound herself. In addition Luis's patriarchal story awakened the father archetype that Carmen had been unconsciously responding to in the relationship to her husband/father.

As a result Carmen, like so many Latinas, realized that she was still living the inherited drama of patriarchy in the way of life of emanation. It was a shock to realize that she was still at home in act I, scene 1. Carmen did leave with her husband to live on the West Coast; but Carmen did not take a journey on the deeper level of her life. To deal with her pain Carmen became a full-time parent in order to give herself a reason for living. But somebody has to pay the price for a woman having to give up her life. For this reason Carmen had to work against violent feelings to get revenge on her husband. Many Latinas are reluctant to admit to this because it is so painful. A spin-off of patriarchy is the repression of anger that breeds more anger and resentment. The kind of anger that is necessary is one that allows people to generate the courage and energy to rebel, to polarize, to break out, to enter into act II, scene 1 as a preparation for emptying oneself of destructive dramas.

For all of these reasons the stories of our lives played out unconsciously—whether in the life of emanation, incoherence, or deformation—are so crippling and ultimately devoid of transformative justice. Appeals to loyalty, power, or violence are useless in the face of having to change one's life on the deeper level. Only in the service of transformation does one have the insight, love, analytical ability, and understanding to participate in building a fundamentally more just and rewarding life for all members of the family.

For generations in the Latino culture, men and women, like Luis and Carmen, stayed together for the sake of the children, because of religious reasons, to avoid the shame that ending the marriage would bring, or because of the established ethos that a woman never abandons her family. In these instances the archetypal drama of patriarchy possesses them in act I, scene 1 in the way of life of emanation; they do not have a marriage, the marriage has them. In order to break this archetypal drama, divorce becomes a viable alternative. If two persons cannot or will not resolve the problems that they brought to the marriage, then the relationship will get worse. Sexuality becomes a duty, or an inconvenience that has to be accommodated. Such passionless unions become economic, contractual agreements wherein daily tasks like shopping, going to a movie, or doing housework are performed in a businesslike manner. As a result the marriage may be reformed into a contractual agreement in the way of life of incoherence.[3] Possessive love gives way to power relations; but intimacy, being close to oneself and being vulnerable to others, is just as impossible as in the way of life of emanation.

For many Latino males like Luis, the archetypal drama of patriarchy, the possessive mother, the dramas of jealous love, violence, and immaturity led to many unsatisfactory relationships with women. Wounded by matriarchy, the other face of patriarchy, Luis came to realize that he had married his mother in the guise of his wife. Because the wife takes the place of the mother Luis was anxious to be with other women to get away from this troubling fusion of mother and wife. He looked for relationships with other women but often felt guilty and so returned to the family as a return to innocence. Many Latinas, like Carmen, responded to these infidelities by deadening their feelings. This emotional detachment has left many marriages cold and empty and always bordering on anger at the slightest provocation.

Carmen responded to Luis's affairs in various ways: confusion hurt, denial, rage, resignation, depression, and, finally, a decision to cut herself off emotionally so that no matter what Luis did it would no longer hurt her. They both had to work at being civil to each other. Thus repression always leads to denying and actually killing one's emotions and sexuality. This kind of living is in the service of deformation. Life becomes fundamentally worse. The partial selves of Luis and Carmen could not be healed by living the story of patriarchy in the service of emanation or by power plays enacted in the service of the way of life of incoherence. The failure of these two ways of life often leads to deformation.

Luis and Carmen's decision to stay together did not protect the children. The frustration of the marriage led to abusive behavior against them. Luis was continuing in his own family the physical abuse that he had experienced and that he had vowed never to do. Carmen was almost immobilized in the face of patriarchal authority; she desperately wanted to come to the defense of the children but the story of patriarchy overwhelmed her. Carmen became increasingly angry with her life and the powerlessness that froze her. After twenty years she commented that she still found it very difficult to resist Luis's verbal abuse against their youngest daughter. Further discussion led to the revelation that Carmen could not talk with her father about anything meaningful. She recalls as a young woman looking at her father across the table and being amazed that she could be so intimidated by this man. This remembrance by Carmen is a powerful testimony to the presence of the mysterious and the sacred in the stories of our lives. Carmen was overwhelmed not by her own, actual father but by the underlying archetype of the father that gave her father his mysterious power to dominate her so completely.

Carmen began to fight back; she went back to school and got a very good paying job. The children were pleased to see their mother independent. Carmen now began to practice the forbidden relationships of boundary management and isolation that threatened the Latino inherited relationships of dependency, especially emanation and subjection. However, the children were often upset to see the harshness that surfaced between their parents.

The issue for Latino families, as it is for Luis and Carmen, is to ask if they can afford to continue to pay the heavy price exacted by the story of patriarchy. The emotional cost, as both Carmen and Luis experienced, is unbearable. As we have witnessed, the children were severely hurt, both physically and emotionally.

THE ARCHETYPE OF POSSESSIVE LOVE

There is a further dimension of the patriarchal drama: possessive love. Luis and the majority of men from all cultural backgrounds cannot conceive of their wives ever being married to or living with another man. It was unthinkable that Latina women could have a sexual life of their own apart from their husbands. Yet Luis admitted that he could see himself married to another woman. There is a deep voice in Latino men that says my wife belongs to me as a total possession. Intellectually many Latino men, especially the young and better educated, do not believe this, but it is the archetypal drama of male/female relationships in the service of the dying way of life of emanation that possesses them. Staying married is one way to continue to possess a woman and to persist in fending off the relationship of incoherence, the act of rebellion in act II, scene 1. Possessive love actually goes berserk in the face of the slightest resistance. Physical assaults, or the threat of such attacks, is always present as a deterrent.

Currently Luis and Carmen are confronting possessive love enacted in the drama of patriarchy together and with their children. They have begun family therapy. They realize that it will not be easy. They have no idea as to where this will lead them, but they do know they cannot go back. In long and honest conversations they are exposing how the drama of patriarchy inflicted their lives. There is no question that they have entered act II, scene 1 together, a scene wherein they have broken with the inherited patriarchal drama and possessive love of the Latino family in the service of emanation. Now the more difficult struggle faces them: entering act II, scene 2 and emptying themselves of the archetypal, underlying story of patriarchy that controlled their lives. They are often afraid and at times they slip back into living fragments of the way of life of emanation. They are no longer naive about the effort that will be necessary to free themselves from destructive dramas. We will return to the struggle of Carmen and Luis to actually empty themselves of destructive archetypal stories in Chapter Five.

THE ARCHETYPAL DRAMA OF MATRIARCHY

For years I have been puzzled by the central place that women play in the Latino culture and community and yet their subservience to men. What I have come to discover is that matriarchy was a historical response to the needs of the Latino family in the urban, industrialized society of the United States and in the cities of Latin America. In reality matriarchy was a rebellious response to the drama of patriarchy.[4] For centuries in Latin America our foremothers exercised covert manipulation. Latinas subtly controlled a man by giving him the impression that he was in control while she got her own way. This is an arrested form of rebellion that makes it impossible to get beyond act II, scene 1. We cannot enter act II, scene 2 and empty ourselves of the drama of patriarchy and of the way of life of emanation.

Patriarchy is reformed with a female face and thus becomes matriarchy: "I am a woman. I am in charge." In this scenario women still accept the inevitability of domination on the basis of gender and try to make it less oppressive. By their success some actually strengthened and prolonged male domination. By not attacking the very heart of patriarchy, which is rooted in the assertion of one gender's inferiority, women participated in oppression. To continue to live this story with women now in charge meant that women became rebels; they now did to men what had been done to them, which means that their lives were controlled by the story of the oppressor. Many other Latinas perpetuated the story of patriarchy by participating in covert manipulation. By telling men what they wanted to hear and then doing what they planned to do all along, women were still deferring to men. This means that the same drama of domination is being lived; this strategy allows everyone to continue to live in a fog of false consciousness that persists in wounding the Latino community.

In this country matriarchy underwent a dramatic change. Latino families, and especially the mothers, played a crucial role for first- and second-generation Latinos. Utter survival in the worst of circumstances meant using a great deal of affection, buffering, and isolating from the larger and dangerous world of power in the service of incoherence. The intent was to hang on to the inherited, rural life in the way of life of emanation as a form of continuity in the midst of so much change. As a result Latina women were willing to put up with almost anything to protect their children and husbands.

In these dire circumstances most Latino men still held onto the privileges of patriarchy. Latina women were reared in the way of life of emanation to prepare themselves to receive suffering, disappointment, and pain from their husbands. Their joy was their children and the family. They were raised not to consider their own desires and dreams as important. In order to preserve the cosmic hierarchy of husbands, priests, male deities, and their fixed gender role, Latina women repressed their own feelings, dreams, and ideas.

It is on this repression that so many children were able to be protected in a hostile society. As discussed, the Latina woman usually
enacted her life in the service of the way of life of emanation. And
while it helped the family to survive in a hostile environment, for
both women and men the price was their inability to create alternative female/male relationships or families in the service of transformation.

THE NAVARRETTE FAMILY

In the Navarrette family, which represents five generations, four
born in this country (roughly covering the years 1922 to the
present), there are lawyers, nurses, engineers, teachers, doctors, and
businesswomen and -men. Thus the repression necessary for patriarchy to work and the compensatory matriarchal love for family
became the matrix out of which so much reformation but not transformation came forth. This fact points out the power of archetypal
dramas. The majority of the children came forth as more powerful
extensions of their parents because they were also cleverly able to
use the new power relations of the new society.

However, although Latina mothers and grandmothers maintained the stability and continuity of the family and were largely
responsible for keeping the home as a source of protection, the time
for enacting the archetypal drama of matriarchy as a means of
survival in the service of emanation is over. To be successful in a
new country that did not respect their culture and community,
Latina mothers created a matriarchy precisely to protect the patriarchy. Latino males had to be protected from the racism and
unemployment that undermined their sense of dignity and respect.

In fact, the external attack of the wider society made Latina
women more protective of the family. They believed this was not
a time for internal family challenges when the whole culture was
endangered. Thus the drama and relationships of the way of life of
emanation were maintained as a defense mechanism. As harsh as
it may seem to say, most of the women and men refused to take
the risk of transformation. Yet people have to start where they are.
As a community Latinos cannot wait until they are college graduates
or rich or powerful in order to transform their lives.

Increasingly Latinos realized that there were alternatives, that their inherited way of life was not the only one and that what was demanded was change. But what kind of change? Some families encouraged bilingualism and biculturalism; others urged that their children forget Spanish and accommodate themselves to this country. Some Latino parents refused to be bicultural or to assimilate; they stubbornly held their distance from this society as an attempt to continue the inherited way of life of emanation in this society and demanded that their children do the same.

What was at stake in all of this maneuvering was the competing ways of life of emanation and incoherence. The Navarrette family of five generations was responding in a variety of ways. Individual members from different family branches and from different generations responded to problems differently. Some of the family spoke Spanish, some refused to; others identified with Mexicans/Latinos, while a few tried to pass as Anglos. Many have married European-Americans and so the language of the culture was further threatened. What held all of these responses together was the matriarch. At Christmas, or her birthday, or the wedding anniversary all revolved around the matriarch, the grandmother, by now a great- and great-great-grandmother.

It was love, respect, and affection for her that held the various family branches together. Those who could not relate to each other because of differences in values, life-style, or age, related through her as the mediatrix. Matriarchs knew in their bones that this was their source of emanational power. They encouraged, rebuked softly, provided money, guidance, and advice. Money was often passed on the sly without the knowledge of the grandfather or father to those in need. Over the years this kind of nurturing was reciprocated by the young as they found their place in life.

The death of the Navarrette family's matriarch, as well as other Latina matriarchs who were the first generation of Latinas in this country, leaves Latinos alone and bereft with a sense of vulnerability, not just as individuals, but as a people, a community, a family. As the matriarchs, who are now in their eighties, die there is nobody to take their place. It is as if the spell is broken. Christmas is no longer the same: the mounds of gifts that surrounded Latina grandmothers as the family paid homage cannot be replicated by the patriarch. His emanational power, already damaged by this society, is now almost gone as the younger generation gets further away from the old stories of the migration, unemployment, discrimination, and hard times. The family becomes families in the service of different ways of life.

The matriarchs did their job well. The best of them showed the reformative face of the great mother archetype. They were and are mothers who, often at great risk to themselves, protected their families during times of great need. Now survival in the service of emanation must be enacted in the service of transformation. The way of emanation cannot endure problems of a fundamentally new kind. Emanation as a holding pattern until families got settled and as a buffer from the way of life of incoherence and deformation was a service done out of love and commitment. But now many have outgrown emanation as a way of life, not because they are not grateful but because they have realized the terrible price of this way of life and they are asking new questions and making choices that contradict the inherited ways of an unbreakable web of life.

Many Latinos are growing new dramas and relationships that protect the individuality of men and women and family simultaneously. Therefore, survival as an archetype is being acted out in new ways that demand a new self, politics, history, and face of the sacred. Today, survival must not be reduced to assimilation or settling for less in the service of incoherence. The way of life of incoherence permanently arrested in act II, scene 1 destroys community, compassion, service, love, and the self as sacred. Everyone is processed as a fragment and no one knows the other in their wholeness. Nor should the need for survival be allowed to become a justification for the murder of Latino youth and community by turning to drugs or drug-related profits. Today, more than ever before, to survive one must *sobrevivir*, which means not just mere survival but to succeed, to surpass, to overcome the inherited past and the temptation to assimilate in order to create in the service of transformation.

To grow one's own family in the service of transformation will take many forms. Due to the weakening of the dramas of patriarchy/matriarchy, and the problems in the wider society, many in the community, especially the poor, desperately need family. But what kind of family and in what ultimate service will they be called upon to put it in place? As argued above, the way of life of emanation is almost gone, especially with the passing of the matriarchs. Incoh-

erence as a way of life that inspires the pursuit of power has not
succeeded in providing Latinos and people of color with a viable
alternative. Desperation has led too many Latinos to forms of deformation in which they lose themselves and others in self-hatred
and hatred of the Anglo world.

The only workable alternative is to create responses to each other
in the service of transformation. The choice of this way of life will
have an immediate impact on the Latino family: it will enable all
to see the frightening price of emanational repression. Men and
women as parents or single parents will survive only to the extent
that they see each other as mutual—as friend, lover, brother, sister,
father, daughter, colleague, companion. Children need to be reared
as persons so that they become participatory selves, individuals in
the community prepared to struggle with family and community in
a democratic process.

One of the immediate challenges to the Latino family is that the
children might lose contact with their Latino heritage. But what
Latinos must hang on to above all is the story of the journey to
this country, which is symbolic of the journey of transformation
on the deeper archetypal levels that all need to take time and again.
This readiness to journey, to struggle, to rear new generations who
care about the human family as *La Raza* is the challenge. This is
not a utopian ideal. We need this kind of thinking and action today.
At times Latinos who speak Spanish perfectly and stay in contact
with their roots might do so to gain political office in the pursuit
of self-interest in the way of life of incoherence.

Many Latinos who refuse to speak Spanish and reject their culture
out of shame have not willingly chosen this impoverishment but
may become aware of their loss and rediscover their heritage. Some
Latinos who no longer speak Spanish well are deeply committed
to justice in the community and act on its behalf. The issue here is
who are our brothers and sisters, nieces, mothers, fathers?—those
who practice transformation as a way of living. Therefore, European-Americans and people of color who practice the heresy of
continuous creation and who care deeply about matters of justice
are also members of the family, *El Pueblo*.

In the years ahead Latinos are going to need new ways of creating,
nourishing, and dissolving in order to plan new families. This is a
difficult task because no society has really done this before. This

means to break new ground. Yet this is precisely the spirit of hope with which Latino foremothers and forefathers left their home and came to this nation. Latina mothers often said that they had come here out of love for their husbands and to nurture their family. Can the present generation do any less? Out of love, yes, but a new love in the service of transformation that discerns and confronts the needs of the time is the thread from which to create new families for a dawning age.

This, then, is the heart of the Latino family's dilemma: they did not ask for the archetypal wounding found in the story of patriarchy; they inherited this from their culture, history, and society. However, now that more Latinos are conscious of these archetypal dramas, they are fully responsible for the quality of life within their families. Therefore they are not victims but people in need of each other and of their deepest sources. Latinos have to struggle with their selves, their culture; they are responsible for critiquing and breaking destructive, inherited archetypal dramas that suck them into an abyss of anger and death. The people are the living stones of the culture and therefore have the right to discover and nourish the positive and to empty themselves of the destructive stories of the culture.

It has been argued that the diversity in Latino families is due to issues such as immigration patterns, class, intermarriage, urbanization, generational issues, industrialization, regional differences, and discrimination. Certainly these are very important issues in the life of any family. Urbanization became a problem for Latinos because it displaced them from the land and forced them into the market economy, wherein the way of life of incoherence is dominant. The inherited way of emanation was further undermined by the introduction of a competing way of life and, new, created, concrete manifestations of previously forbidden archetypal patterns and dramas.

Nevertheless, many families, and especially women, experienced economic autonomy for the first time and this led them to challenge the domination of men. Some women and men responded to the challenge and successfully emptied themselves of patriarchy and of the way of life of emanation by entering act II, scene 2 and creating new manifestations of archetypal relationships with their families in act III, scenes 1 and 2 in the service of transformation. For this reason we cannot do sweeping statistical studies that generalize based on external changes. The changes that count are those that take place in our deepest depths, which lead to personal, political, historical, and sacred changes.

Good theory allows us to see recurring patterns; but, in addition, archetypal analysis requires us to recognize that if dramas and especially our four, ultimate, overarching ways of life change, then a revolution in the depths and in our daily lives is in the making. There is no escape from doing constant archetypal analysis so that we may catch relationships, dramas, ways of life, and the source of all sources in motion. The conflict between culturally inherited Latino values—that is, the fragments of the way of life of emanation and the economic pressures of this industrialized, urban society dominated by the way of life of incoherence—is the confrontation and competition between two ways of life that exist side by side in the souls of the people as well as externally in the body politic.

Archetypal analysis allows Latinos to disentangle these ways of life and to recognize the limits of both since they are unfinished, truncated aspects of the core drama of transformation. To choose either the way of emanation or incoherence or a mixture of the two will eventually end in failure. In neither way of life can a person persistently, if at all, ask new kinds of questions and create necessary responses. The logic and limits of these two ways does not allow the emergence of fundamentally new and more just relationships and dramas. Therefore the community faces more incoherence as they demand of these ultimate ways of life answers that they cannot provide. The ensuing sense of loss leaves Latinos vulnerable to a more serious underlying eruption of deformational sources that will pull them into a whirlpool of despair.

In the personal deepest self, the sacred, archetypal sources are never in a state of equilibrium. We, together with these sources, persistently participate in the dialectic of destroying, creating, and nourishing. To attempt to preserve or freeze a particular moment is to try to suppress the source, which cannot be done. To fail to actively engage the sources is to become possessed by them. To dare to command the sources is to commit that hubris of which the Greeks warned. The most fruitful response is to choose from among the competing archetypal ways and to elect the way of life of transformation. This way of life and the god of transformation

eagerly awaits and invites our participation. Therefore, unlike Cal-
vinist doctrine, all are elected and in turn can elect transformation,
the only source that can guide and help us draw from our own
deepest wells, the source of all sources, the god beyond god.

   In the context of this book we have met different lords in the
depths and seen their impact in the day-to-day reality of the Latino
family. In telling the archetypal drama of the Latino family I am
also telling, and thereby rediscovering, my own story. My hope is
that what I write will strike a resonating chord in the lives and
stories of Latinas and Latinos as well as others from all ethnic and
cultural backgrounds. A good teacher, poet, artist, or novelist does
not deposit anything in us as if we were an empty shell; our finest
teachers, poets, artists, and storytellers put into words, colors,
shades, hues, and nuance what we have always had within us. By
telling their stories they help us to uncover our lives, help us to
come forth out of ourselves and empower us to tell our own
stories in our own unique ways.

   I am especially drawn to the work of Sandra Cisneros, who in
her latest work, *Woman Hollering Creek* (a collection of stories),
is creating a whole new understanding of what it means to be a
Latina woman.[5] Cisneros is challenging a five-hundred-year-old tradition of the Latina woman as permanent victim: *la llorona*, the
woman who wanders the streets throughout Latin America crying
out for her lost children. There are various interpretations of this
story. Some say that it represents the violated and abandoned
women of Latin America; others that it symbolizes the unforgettable
trauma of the Conquest and the loss of Native American identity.
I believe that Cisneros is deliberately challenging this central story/
myth of a violated womanhood/identity/culture and attempting to
create a new sense of self, politics, history, and sacred story for
Latina women. It is not an exaggeration to claim that what Cisneros
is doing is rejecting *la llorona*, the woman crying and overwhelmed
with grief because it stereotypes excluded groups, and especially
women, as permanent victims. "Woman Hollering" in Spanish is
gritona, not just *a* woman but the new human condition of woman
as shouter, protestor, dissenter. This is a fundamental departure
from women who cry out but who also submit to their fate. In the
story "Woman Hollering Creek," Cleofilas makes a political move
by leaving an abusive husband; in so doing she breaks a historical

pattern and initiates a new story for Latina women. By so doing she asserts the sacredness and value of a woman's life. Virtue is no longer submissiveness as the lords of emanation demand but the call of the journey is an invitation from the god of transformation to begin a new life.

CONCLUSION

This is what constitutes a true politics of the family: consciously, mutually, lovingly choosing how to relate to one another, emptying oneself of the destructive stories, and creating afresh in the service of the way of life of transformation. What better way is there to prepare children to grow their own personhood? How better to relativize the power of institutions and to demonstrate that our marriages, families, schools, churches, culture, and society consist of our relationships to one another. Institutions are human ways of relating and therefore belong to us to be uprooted when inadequate so that new ones may take root and grow.

Latinos have to be serious about the business of growing their own families. As I understand this process, it means the refusal to be assimilated and socially adjusted into the official ethos of a white, middle-class culture arrested in act II, scene 1 of the core drama in the way of life of incoherence. This does not mean a rejection of white or European-American people, but of white attitudes—that is, their story that is based on power and exclusion. Thus to say no to assimilation is not to be anti-Anglo but to stand against the pursuit of self-interest and power in the service of incoherence. Power of its very nature is scarce and therefore must exclude, dominate, and even kill, thus increasingly ending in the practice of deformation. For this reason as people of color we cannot assimilate but rather insist on creating more just and compassionate relationships in the service of transformation. In effect this means also breaking with many aspects of the inherited Latino past. Assimilation is not the answer but neither is the search for a golden past nor striking out against others in retaliation. *Boricua*, *Latino*, *La Raza*, and *Chicano* are words that represent a political decision to create a new peoplehood, a new identity for Latinos in the service of transformation.

If this is so, then Latinas and Latinos must resist adopting a married and family life-style that represses their spontaneity, affection, and warmth. As marriage partners, people can have their autonomy and self-development without sacrificing the best that is within their heritage. Let me give an example. Two mothers kiss their children tenderly and with great affection. However, one woman kisses her child to possess her and preserve her in act I, scene 1, while the other gives love to prepare her child for the day when she must leave and begin her journey by entering into act I, scene 2 and breaking relationships of dependence and entering into act II, scene 1. The exact same exterior act is involved, a sign of affection, but it is radically transformed in the one case by the conscious intent of the mother, by the quality of the relationship involved. The former uses affection to perpetuate dependence, in our theoretical language, in the service of emanation, whereas the latter mother enacts love in the service of transformation. Unless Latinos take the risk of breaking the inadequate and often violent relationships they now maintain, members of the family will not be free to transform themselves or the society. The revolution must take place in the depths.

NOTES

1. Gerda Lerner, *The Creation of Patriarchy* (New York: Oxford University Press, 1986), pp. 218–19. Also in regard to understanding how patriarchy permeates the whole of a culture's life—its personal, political, historical, and sacred faces—see Hisham Sharabi's excellent work, *Neopatriarchy: A Theory of Distorted Change in Arab Society* (New York: Oxford University Press, 1988). Another benefit of this book is that it provides a good insight into the failure of patriarchy to reestablish itself as neopatriarchy in a new world that no longer supports this drama with the aura of invincibility as the will of Allah.

2. Lerner, *The Creation of Patriarchy*, p. 219.

3. Irene I. Blea, *La Chicana and the Intersection of Race, Class, and Gender* (New York: Praeger, 1992). I disagree with Ms. Blea's statement that prior to the colonization of the Southwest by the United States following the U.S./Mexican War that Chicanos enjoyed interdependent male/female relationships. Even prior to the Conquest the indigenous peoples were hierarchically organized with the male priestly and warrior castes at the top of the social structure. Latina women were the victims of the story

of patriarchy long before the coming of the Europeans, and too many women and men of the Latino heritage continue to suffer from this drama.

4. See, in regard to very good sources on the story of matriarchy, Lerner, *The Creation of Patriarchy*, p. 250.

5. Sandra Cisneros, *Woman Hollering Creek* (New York: Random House, 1991).

Chapter Four

The Latino Family at Risk

We must be able to identify the problem—that is, inherited relationships, archetypal dramas, usually enacted in the three truncated ways of life of emanation, incoherence, and deformation that have shaped the Latino family. It is necessary to analyze the effects of this cultural heritage so that Latinos neither romanticize nor stereotype their past. Latinos must reaffirm the family but be prepared to grow a new kind of family that empowers both men and women to step forward as equals in the sacred task of preparing the next generation of Latinos. At the same time the wider society must be made accountable for the frightful cost to the community because of its neglect.

Today Latino families are in great danger. Many are surrounded by the dramas of incoherence and deformation that threaten to destroy the moral fiber of their lives. Latino children are increasingly born into a world without the merciful container of security to which all children have a right. Because of the breakdown of male/female and husband/wife relationships in the Latino family, many children are badly hurt. The future of the family is being threatened as never before because too many children are being born into the abyss of poverty, racism, drugs, and AIDS that the society at large refuses in most instances to address.

The Latino family does not live in a vacuum; as an institution it is experiencing both an internal breakdown and an external assault. The first three chapters have provided an analysis as to why the Latino family is in trouble due to the breaking of inherited concrete manifestations of the archetypal relationships of emanation, subjection, isolation, buffering, and direct exchange in the service of emanation. Latinos are questioning the archetypal dramas into which they were socialized, especially those of patriarchy, matriarchy, possessive love, and the woman as permanent victim. They are witnessing the dying of the way of life of emanation as well as the fragility and powerlessness of the ways of life of incoherence and deformation.

The destruction of the way of life of emanation and its effects are still being felt, especially in regard to the future of the family and male/female relationships in the Latino community. Coming to the United States was not the most serious experience of incoherence; it was the Conquest that initiated a whole series of scars that are still being felt. Just as individuals suffer traumas that affect them the rest of their lives, in like manner whole communities, nations, and cultures can also be traumatized. Octavio Paz argues in an essay, "Sons of La Malinche," that the indigenous male, in what is now Latin America, at the time of the Conquest was deeply wounded.[1] The males saw their women and children ravaged and often killed and they could do nothing. However, the greatest shock came when women like La Malinche, an Aztec woman, actually betrayed the people and sided with the Spaniards. La Malinche was renamed Doña Maria and became the mistress of Cortes. To this day, if you are called a Malinchista in Mexico, you are guilty of betrayal.[2]

Aztec males considered their women to be passive, open, and too docile in the face of the enemy. Yet this is the way the women had been reared in their own culture in the way of life of emanation. But now this openness was used as an excuse against them to deflect the blow to the male's pride. Women became known as *chingadas*, a very difficult term to translate but which in that historical context meant a woman who was violated, deceived, and forcibly opened. The children of the violated women were *los hijos de la chingada*, the offspring of deception and rape.

This traumatic experience also seems to have given a more desperate grasping to Native American *machismo*, an inherited visceral right and desire of males to dominate women; in the context of the Conquest it represents a desperate effort to reassert identity and culture. The Conquest constituted an overwhelming sense of loss. A world died and a new one dominated by foreigners was being constructed. Both the Spaniard and the indigenous male were patriarchal, but in attempting to regain their lost identity Native American males emphasized the possession of the women. So Indian men took on the characteristics of the oppressor. The father stepped forward aggressively because his patriarchal identity was threatened; he wanted to continue not only to love in a possessive manner but to overpower as was his right given to fathers in the story of patriarchy in the way of life of emanation.

It was a rebellious response to a sense of having fallen from grace. To be born a male was to be obligated to prove your ability to be the source of mystery in the lives of others and to dominate. Crippled in the public realm, the men exercised power with few restraints or limits in the privacy of their domestic domain. The masculine deities were defeated by the Spaniards, especially Huitzilopochtli, the god of war, and Quetzalcoatl, the god of culture. This marked the end of an era, a cosmic cycle was shattered, and a new divine kingdom was inaugurated that emphasized ancient feminine deities. Even the Virgen de Guadalupe was not seen as an earth goddess who represented the rhythm of the seasons and agrarian rites; she was a source of refuge where the people could hide and try to recover from the trauma.

Therefore, the feminine suffered a terrible setback in the Latin American psyche. The feminine is considered to be docile and weak in the face of trouble. La Malinche, although peculiarly Mexican, becomes symbolic of women throughout Latin America. To reject women is, therefore, an attempt to deny the past, the traumatic origins, and to choose to live in a stoic solitude. Even *mestizaje*, the miscegenation of peoples, is a curse because it represents the mixture of blood and culture that was not mutual but imposed by a people who considered themselves superior. Thus, many Latinos live with a great ambivalence owing to this traumatic experience that is often repressed. They are so close to their roots and yet are often ashamed of their past.

In the language of the theory of transformation, Latin America suffered a destruction of the way of life of emanation. Many in-

digenous people shifted their loyalty to the Spaniards, just as they
had on other occasions to other conquering groups. They thus
attempted to reform the incoherence of the conquest into another
substitute way of life of emanation. This was not a transformation
but a reformation. In the public realm, the conquered population
was baptized and became loyal vassals of the Spanish king. Yet
underneath there was a resistance that did not allow uncritical
loyalty that is characteristic of the way of life of emanation. This
leads to the conclusion that for five centuries two competing ways
of life of emanation coexisted: one a loyal attempt to hang on to
the cultural values of the past, and the other a leap into the European, Catholic melting pot. Often not even the Spaniards or the
Native American population, now rapidly becoming *mestizo* (a
blend of the two) was aware of this split personality.

Just as this cultural ambivalence remains to this day, so too does
the distrust of women, and not only of women, but more important,
a fear and suspicion of the feminine. This rejection of the feminine
is far more serious because it means that not only can Latino men
not relate to women as equals but they cannot accept the feminine
aspects of their own personalities. This confusion often leads to a
cultural and political denigration of women. This, in turn, reinforces
gender roles, perpetuates the story of patriarchy, and turns Latino
males into potential abusers.

CAUGHT BETWEEN TWO WAYS OF LIFE

Immigration to the United States does not heal but deepens the
ambivalent anxiety of the Latino male. Once again, many are threatened by white males and see Latina women as potential victims and
betrayers. Since there is fear, *machismo* is aroused. As in the urban
centers of Latin America, people might practice new forms of relationship in the public realm but often maintain inherited patterns
of relating in the realm of the family. In U.S. society what is necessary is aggressiveness and competition, which is made concrete
by the relationships of isolation, direct exchange, and boundary
management. These new relationships are learned by Latinas and
Latinos but they continue to live with fragments of the way of life
of emanation that provides a form of buffering that hides the deeper
traumatic experiences that have not healed. This, I suspect, is why

so many Latino men are stoic and taciturn about their personal lives. But when they drink, the hurt, confusion, and being torn between ways of life come pouring forth. Latinos are looking for ways of expressing, of confessing so that they can break out of their solitude and anger.

In addition to the historical trauma of the Conquest, the loss of the way of life of emanation and their archetypal stories have left Latinos very vulnerable to the official way of life of U.S. society, to the service of incoherence, and to the ever-growing danger of new forms of deformation. Economic fears have triggered a deep anxiety in U.S. society that the middle class will lose what small gains it has made during the past ten years. The rich and powerful complain that this country is going in the wrong direction. These feelings of dis-ease persist in spite of the fact that the richest 1 percent of our population has been rewarded with a remarkable 70 percent raise in real dollars since 1978 due to benefits from the tax structure.[3]

For the powerful, there are only two kinds of people, as Frances Fox Piven and Richard Cloward have described, either entrepreneurs or malingerers. The whole strategy of the supply-side people was to reward the entrepreneurs so that with their expertise and energy new jobs, industries, and growth would come. To the so-called malingerers the message was clearly sent in the form of cutbacks that totaled many billions of dollars in social services. The attitude behind this hard line was that the welfare state had made it too easy for people to be unemployed.[4] If benefits were cut it would force people into the work force to provide an army of low-paid, nonunionized workers with poor benefits and with little or no chance of advancement. The jobs being created were primarily in the service sector. Meanwhile, manufacturing jobs were and are disappearing to overseas locations and with them the power of the unions to exercise direct bargaining power with the corporations has also gone. There is another aspect to the loss of union power: it is a political issue because workers cannot join together in order to preserve rights obtained through sacrifices made in the past.

This kind of change in the economy directly affects Latinos as the largest and latest group of immigrants arriving daily in the United States. Schooling is more essential than ever because of the shift away from manufacturing to high-tech jobs and yet the average dropout rate for Latino high school students is close to 50 percent throughout the country. Thus Latino youth will be condemned to low-paying, nonunionized jobs with poor benefits.[5] When my father arrived in this country from Michoacan, Mexico, he didn't need to know English to get a good union job with the United Auto Workers at Ford. But today this is a different world and time.

The need for education also requires a particular kind of schooling in bilingual/bicultural studies that can give Latino youth a chance to survive in the schools. But once again funds were cut that affected staying in high school, while monies for higher education were simultaneously reduced, thus making it more difficult for those Latinos who finished high school to go to college. However, even if they got to college, they entered campuses that treated them as marginal students who really didn't deserve to be there on merit. In addition many universities and colleges have an attitude about them: "You need us, we don't need you." The hidden political agenda, the invisible curriculum, is too often to turn Latino students into white, middle-class students. The basis for this view is the lack of courses in the curriculum that give Latinos an opportunity to know and celebrate their culture and heritage, and none, or very few, Latino faculty or administrators on the campus. Many Latinos are hired on "soft money" (nonrenewable grants intended to fund remedial work).[6]

The actual income of Latinos, especially among Puerto Ricans, has dropped since the 1980 Census. We now have Latino families on welfare into the third generation. The lack of access to quality education, jobs, housing, and health have combined to create a ring of exclusion around U.S. society.[7] Affirmative Action and Equal Employment Opportunity were put on hold and weakened throughout the Reagan/Bush years. Recently Jules Feiffer, the political cartoonist, gave his assessment of U.S. society and spoke of the nation as "moving towards armed camps."[8]

The FBI has reported on an alarming emergence of right-wing groups in the country. What makes this even more disturbing was the coalition-building going on among groups such as the Ku Klux Klan, the American Aryan Party, and other right-wing organizations. Other less-threatening, but nevertheless discriminatory, groups have emerged such as the English Only Movement, which has experienced legislative successes in thirteen states including Cal-

ifornia and Nevada. Bills to make English the official and only
language by which to conduct government business are pending in
thirty-seven state legislatures.

The erection of industrial parks and shopping malls, far removed
from the inner cities, is another factor leading to the perception of
the United States as moving toward two societies: one, white and
privileged; the other, people of color who are excluded from the
benefits of society. Latinos who do not have private transportation
in personal autos cannot go to work in these malls and parks. Public
transportation is almost nonexistent and that which exists means
adding three to four hours to their work day. When jobs are found,
they are of a menial nature. High-paying secretarial positions are
often filled by the wives of executives. There is no child care available, adding to the hardship of young couples or single parents who
have to work to support the family.

Prenatal care for the poor was drastically cut. This, of course,
often leads to low-birth-weight children, because the mothers suffer
from poor diets and inadequate medical care. In many cases the
combination of poor nutrition and lack of access to medical facilities
has caused serious health problems that are even more costly for
the family and, eventually, the society at large.[9]

The consequence of all of these difficulties for the poor means
that the ways of life of incoherence and deformation are alarmingly
prevalent in our society. The pursuit of power by those arrested in
act II, scene I of the core drama in the service of incoherence is
insatiable; caught in the logic of this way of life, people never have
enough money or power. The conscious exclusion of the poor,
people of color, and other unprotected groups means that the poor
are dying before their time.[10] This is an enactment of the way of
destructive death, of the drama of tribalism in the service of deformation; some are made expendable *because* of their ethnicity,
race, gender, or class.

Perhaps the most dangerous drama of deformation for the Latino
community and the family today is the emergence of the drug culture, which offers immediate adventure, a perpetual high, un-
dreamed of amounts of money, power, and influence. There is
something of great historical significance taking place in the United
States at this time. Drugs, we know, have been used for centuries
in religious ceremonies and for healing purposes. To this day in

Yemen, Bolivia, and Peru, people chew gut or coca leaves as a narcotic that helps to shield them against hunger, extreme cold, and the
effects of living at high altitudes. The drugs are a survival mechanism in a fragile world. Latinos, and other excluded groups, in U.S.
society are making a statement when they take drugs—that they are
suffering from severe personal, economic, and cultural dislocation.

For centuries Latinos were ruled both culturally and politically
by *caudillos* (patriarchal leaders). The loss of this type of dominating
leadership, legitimated by the way of life of emanation, created a
crisis of authority. The vacuum that resulted because of the breakdown of authority allows the emergence of the drug dealer, endowed
with an emanational mystique, to become the new *caudillo* who is
dedicated only to destructive death. *Caudillos*, bosses, and paternalistic leaders, in the way of life of emanation, were often the
godfather of many children whose parents were *campesinos* on the
caudillo's land. If there was a bad crop, he made sure that the
people were fed. His personal sense of honor was involved and he
had, in addition, strong emotional bonds with his peons.

This way of ruling was paternalistic and kept the people dependent and poor; but people accepted this as a form of justice that,
although at times harsh, was unavoidable. However, in the ways
of life of incoherence and deformation, this personal sense of responsibility for others is replaced by reducing the people to mere
means for the acquisition of power in the service of incoherence
and the crippling of others in the service of deformation. In reality
this is not a return to a web of security in act I, scene 1, but to a
relationship of emanation in the service of deformation; this relationship of emanation now links followers to powerful drug bosses
who destroy the community for profit. Those who choose to serve
these new *caudillos* enter into a form of deadly rebellion against
white America. To be in rebellion means that they are controlled
by the racist consciousness of those in white America who want
and expect people of color to destroy themselves.

The affluent are also taking drugs, which indicates the pervasive
sense of loss at the heart of U.S. culture. Both suburb and inner
city are engaging in forms of incoherence and deformation as they
fall deeper into possession by drug substances. However, there is a
big difference between drugs in the barrios and in the suburbs. In
the barrios the drugs lead to the destruction of the community itself,

especially the young, who get hooked and are forced to become dealers to support their addiction. In the wealthier areas, the drugs can be more easily paid for if you are a doctor or lawyer. Besides, the suburbs would never stand for crack houses and drug dealers on the street corner.

Nevertheless, in both European-American communities and those of people of color, the pervasive presence of drugs is symptomatic of underlying causes. The way of life of emanation that demanded respect and obedience to authority, as was demonstrated in earlier chapters, is dying. The way of life of incoherence due to its inherent greed cannot allow new forms of justice to include all groups equally in the American dream. The fragility of these two ways of life that arrest us in acts I and II of the core drama becomes more evident each day. This indicates the growing danger of the way of life of deformation that promises a panacea based on a fragment of life such as money, skin color, or gender. This results in the formation of tribalistic camps of perpetually polarized people who consider the other as the enemy.

THE LATINO RESPONSE

Some Latinas and Latinos respond to the stories of powerlessness and death by pursuing power so that they can build a fortress for their own family. In the family's private relationships the father and mother, who have succeeded in doing well, often demands the use of concrete, inherited manifestations of the archetypal relationships within the dying way of life of emanation. The children know the wealth comes from the public realm, where other manifestations of more competitive relationships are employed in the service of a different way of life, that of incoherence. This world has different values and attitudes. This means living a double consciousness and to be caught between two ways of life.

Other Latinos identify their backgrounds with a stigma and blame the Latino culture as weak and defective. This leads to a complete rejection of the way of life of emanation with all of its surrounding characteristics such as honor and respect, Catholic holidays, *La Virgen*, and all other religious and historical earmarks. The only way to be somebody is to be an American. The children are not taught Spanish or any Latino cultural values. The United States is uncritically accepted, in the relationship of emanation, as the best country because it has made Latinos into autonomous individuals with skills and the ability to compete. Thus the relationship of boundary management acquired from the wider society, by which a person becomes, for example, a lawyer, are now used to pursue self-interest and power in the service of incoherence.

The Latinos who remain in the barrios against their will are susceptible to the stories of hopeless death told by AIDS, drugs, liquor, child abuse, and battering of women. Poverty in U.S. society means not having or being excluded from access to the relationships of direct exchange and boundary management. Going to school or college and acquiring skills are what allow people to be marketable. To get a good job you have to have something to bargain with so that you can be placed in a position that demands a strong, competent individual who can defend the boundaries described in the job description. To be denied these two relationships of boundary management and direct exchange in U.S. society is to prevent people from being able to compete; eventually this kind of exclusion based on the greed of the powerful in the service of incoherence can lead to crippling people in the service of deformation. Thus what began as greed leads to destructive death.

This is precisely what poor education, housing, employment, and health effectively accomplish. But the very acceptance of the way of life of incoherence as the answer to the problems of the Latino community is a form of false consciousness. This way of life and the stories that it spawns will make some, and only some, Latinos successful. Seized and caught by the story of power of this way of life, Latinos will refuse to help each other, especially their own poor.

What about the impact of the wider society's structural violence on the Latino community? We know from John Shockley's excellent study, *Chicano Revolt in a Texas Town*, that the Chicanos blamed themselves for their poverty and dire conditions. This was a remarkable victory for the dominators, who were undemocratically controlling the 80 percent of the population who were Latinos. The Anglos in Crystal City had succeeded in getting the Mejicanos to perceive themselves as the Anglos did—as incapable and unworthy to control their own affairs, as inferior people.[11] The Chicanos were caught between the twin towers of death, hatred of self, and hatred of the Anglos. As a people they were caught in the archetypal drama of tribalism because many believed in their own inferiority.

THE FACES OF TRIBALISM/OPPRESSION

Poverty, together with the humiliation of the welfare system and a crippling self-image, has often led to forms of rebellion that spread the dramas of violence and greed in the service of incoherence and deformation. Increasingly we see young Latinos entering into gangs so that they might seek a new kind of family, an extended kinship group with its own language, rituals, and ceremonies. Gangs defend turfs that are considered sacred and members relate to the leader as a source of overwhelming emanation. Within their tribal zones, they have gained control of the drugs, prostitution, numbers, and other payoffs. These young Latinos have actually become rebels in their confrontation with Anglo society. Why rebels? A rebel is a person whose consciousness is being controlled by the story of the persons they despise. They want what the rich have, power; but naively they believe they can get power and revenge without becoming like the oppressors. They have internalized the same stories of destructive death in the service of deformation. These youths have not entered into act II, scene 2, wherein they could empty themselves of the stories of the oppressors. They end by exiting the core drama so that the dominators have won again. Life is not made fundamentally better but worse.

In relationship to the core drama of transformation, such persons exit the core drama. Even though they have rejected the actual, concrete racist/oppressor in their lives in act II, scene 1, they have failed to enter scene 2 and to empty themselves on the deeper level, that of the forming sources, of the story of tribalism, and of the way of life of deformation. Sadly, such persons end up doing to others what was done to them; in this way the same dramas of deformation are repeated. The only thing that changes is the color or language of the oppressor. These youths have taken a fragment of reality, their own ethnicity and cultural heritage, and vested it in a gang, which is a substitute for an extended kinship/family. Their own families and identities were lost with the collapse of the Latino family in the service of emanation as the family attempted to navigate the relationships of power in the way of life of incoherence, or as they confronted the stories of exclusion in the service of deformation that destroyed their hope.

To fight back, many take the fragment of skin color that was considered to be the mark of inferiority and turn it into the sign of superiority. But this is the story of the oppressor; tribalism is tribalism no matter who practices it. The victims now become the victimizers. But once swallowed by this story it dominates its followers. The members of such a gang cannot question or create conflict. They thus murder their intelligence and consciously choose a violent revenge in order to remain loyal to this newfound security in the midst of a crumbling and dangerous world.

MALE/FEMALE RELATIONSHIPS IN THE MIDST OF BREAKDOWN AND DEFORMATION

Increasingly young Latinas caught in the networks of incoherence and deformation affirm life in one of the only ways they feel are left to them, they have children. The child gives them something to live for and, in several interviews that I have seen and read, they state emphatically that the child, above all, will be able to love them. Men, therefore, are seen as a means to an end: pregnancy. But I think that what has happened here it that Latina women, especially if they are the second or third generation in this country, do not want to experience the same fights to be free that they saw their mothers wage against husbands or lovers. Who needs the jealousy, physical intimidation, drinking, womanizing, and double standards of men, they ask. Second- and third-generation Latina women are often different from their mothers because the mothers were raised in the relationships of dependency and strict gender codes of the way of life of emanation. The next generation was not sufficiently socialized in this code of conduct and has had available to it the previously forbidden relationships and ways of life made possible in this society.[12]

Because jobs are not available, school is often going poorly, and there is little to look forward to, the presence of a baby can focus energy, love, commitment, and the future. The Latina woman in such circumstances tends to live totally for her baby. Let us remember that for the most part when we speak of the recent large increase of single parents we are talking about children and young adults twelve to nineteen years old. As children themselves they have not had a chance to test the options of life. Yet this is exactly the point. What options? Born into dire poverty, often deprived of equal access to the acquisition of the relationships of boundary management and direct exchange necessary to survive in this society, often in quarreling families, with the prospect of inferior education and low-paying jobs, the only solution is to secure some goal: a baby, that will provide some meaning in their lives.

This I believe is a search for new forms of emanation. Young Latinas have less and less conscious allegiance to the dying way of life of emanation. Yet they have internalized some of its fragments. Thus when it comes to raising a child they choose the familiar attitudes and relationships of the Latino family, holding on to a person, in this case a baby, in the embrace of emanation. The often-unwed, teenage, single parent believes that the baby will make all the difference. A young mother thus attempts to turn herself into a giver of life in the midst of so much death and failure.

So, in a very real sense this is a rebellion against her own experiences and the society at large: if Latina women reject their heritage they are still living with disappointments that they have not resolved. Therefore, their consciousness is still controlled by fragments of the way of life of emanation. At the same time, in their anger against U.S. society, for having rejected them, they engage in behaviour that will surely, in most cases, condemn them to poverty. In addition, all too often unknown to them, Latina women are repeating the same archetypal relationships and the archetypal drama of their mothers: the story of long-suffering women and dominant men. This means that a young woman is rebelling against men and refuses, or cannot imagine, an intimate, equal relationship as an alternative. Thus they enter into relationships expecting to get hurt and used. At the very least they feel they have the right to get something out of this bargain; a child becomes a possession to be claimed in the relationship of emanation. In the face of so much broken connections in the way of incoherence, they are hoping to build a fortress to protect them in a hostile world and to buffer them from a society that makes them invisible in the way of life of deformation. This child, the Latina believes, will need her alone and love her only for herself.

This example is fraught with the danger that all Latinos will accept the power relationships of the way of life of incoherence as the only way to relate to each other and be tempted by deformation. This acceptance of a lack of a personal commitment as constituting the very fabric of male/female relationships turns encounters into a dance of power that can also turn into a story of deformation. The drama becomes deformational when Latino men react violently to a lover's attempt to become independent, to manipulate them through jealousy or feigned aloofness. If he feels betrayed, this often triggers physical attacks. This reaction is no longer a conscious response on the part of the Latino male. In the drama of possessive love, a man is controlled by the sacred nature of these stories and acts accordingly. Some Latinas in this sadomasochistic drama based on a love/hate dialectic use the Latino male's obsession to get revenge.

Infidelity among Latinos constitutes an adherence to Latino culture in the way of life of emanation. Mediterranean, especially Spanish, culture accepted infidelity as part of life. Within the drama of patriarchy in the service of emanation, a male's faithfulness to infidelity was part and parcel of Latino female/male relationships. Latina women accepted the other woman as part of their fate in the way of life of emanation and resigned themselves to it just as they saw their mothers do the same. Buffers, or ritualized avoidance, were created to veil the presence of the other woman.

Wives almost never brought up the issue because it was considered by all to be a man's right. At times Latinas blamed themselves and decided to lose their sorrows in dedicating themselves to the family. This is exactly what the male wanted because it protected his social, public role as a respected father and husband. In reality it allowed many men to live a double life and to avoid facing their inability to create an intimate, mutual relationship with a woman. Of course this also socialized the children to faithfully carry out their expected gender patterns. It is interesting to note that the famous seventeenth-century Mexican poetess, dramatist, and theologian, Sor Juana Ines de la Cruz, saw only two options for herself as a young woman: to face an arranged, male-dictated married life or go into a convent. She chose the convent because she felt that even within its restrictions she could escape the full weight of the tyranny of male patriarchal domination.[13]

The breakdown of the patriarchal Latino family, arrested in act

I, scene 1 of the core drama in the way of life of emanation, has undermined the justification for infidelity. Latinas, influenced by the wider U.S. society, have for some time now been openly questioning and rejecting the right of a male to infidelity. This situation has led to confrontation in which Latinas, especially because of their increased bargaining power and acquisition of skills—that is, the enacting of the relationships of direct exchange and boundary management—have acquired economic and personal independence usually unknown to their mothers and grandmothers. Economic opportunities and the fight for liberation turned the inherited sexual relationships into encounters of incoherence.

I would like to relate a story to sum up what I have been describing. Several years ago I spoke as the only Latino male present to a group of fifteen Latina women, in Asbury Park, New Jersey. Most of them were young, single parents with sporadic employment. They talked about why they preferred male children who would not have to suffer what they as women have had to endure. They talked about their lives and how they saw Latinas as servants of men.

They realized that in favoring and pampering the boys they were helping to perpetuate the very *machismo* inherent in the story of patriarchy that had hurt them. What they seemed to fear more than anything else, yet felt incapable of preventing, was the possibility that their daughters might end up pregnant, trapped at an early age, eventually tied down with several children, on welfare, and with no options. They realized that their daughters were being condemned to repeat the same dramas that they as their mothers had and were experiencing. Yet they felt that they were powerless.

The sons would continue to be reformed, not transformed into miniature men before their time because they would have to do for their mother what the fathers often refused to do—be loyal, affectionate, and protective. The mothers also knew that they made their sons feel guilty and that they used guilt to bond the child more tightly to themselves. Ironically enough, they expected their sons to be *machos* with women and to "score" but they found a strange consolation in believing that their sons would continue to prefer them before any other woman. They refused to explicitly acknowledge that they were raising their sons to be the next generation of patriarchs.

And yet when they were asked whether or not they were happy, a sad thing happened, almost all of them began to cry. I was deeply moved and left feeling that the conscious articulation and awareness of the stories within which they were trapped were leading to action to reject the inherited story of male domination. In fact, the women in that group were pursuing their high school equivalency certificates and hoped to change their lives for the better.

Being caught in the patriarchal drama for the Latinas referred to in this story consisted of rejecting the husband or boyfriend and yet preferring the male child who would perpetuate the drama. Once again this demonstrates how powerful the stories of our life really are. As sacred dramas they can possess us; even though one breaks with the actual husbands, fathers, lovers, in act II, scene 1, unless they also enter act II, scene 2 and empty themselves of the archetypal drama of patriarchy and the way of life of emanation, this story will return again in the lives of their sons and lovers.

There is another dimension to this story. The Latinas expected to be loved by their children, especially the males, as a fulfillment and reward for all of their sacrifices. However, a young child cannot love a parent as an equal. Because the child will inevitably fail, this expectation can lead to physical punishment, verbal abuse and a corresponding sense of guilt and inadequacy in the son. Unconsciously the son comes to fear his mother's demands and so identifies affection with being swallowed up and devoured. So it is not surprising to find Latino men who are raised in this manner being incapable of relating to women as equals. They cannot be intimate because they feel they have to be on their guard or they will be overwhelmed.

This helps to explain why even though many Latino men have allegedly escaped the sense of shame and sin instilled by their mothers, they end up marrying women who become their mothers. As spoken of above, such Latino males have not succeeded in entering act II, scene 2 of the core drama of transformation, which requires that we not only break with our concrete, specific mother but also in the depths successfully empty ourselves of the archetype of the mother. In this situation matriarchy has replaced patriarchy but again as a rebellion against the dominating male. Whether it is patriarchy or matriarchy, both men and women are crippled because neither of these stories or archetypal dramas allows for the creation of new manifestations in place of the Latino inherited repertory of archetypal relationships nor of an alternative story such as mutuality between men and women in the way of life of transformation.

To hold on to a man our Latina women have often been faithful to them and unfaithful to themselves and their needs as a person. After years of this kind of self-immolation, women can become martyrs who now want others to sacrifice their lives as a debt. Other women become bitter and cynical about love and marriage. This awakening from the nightmare of servanthood in the dying way of life of emanation often leads to breaking with this way of life but then entering into power struggles with men who are now economic providers but not lovers in the way of life of incoherence. Worst of all, other Latina women turn to drugs and alcohol as a form of suicide or to get revenge on their men. This latter choice is a story of deformation where there is no hope.

Some social agencies and workers antagonize the situation by treating Latino families, and especially Latina women, as being defective both morally and culturally. Welfare workers themselves are reduced to being bureaucrats who must process hundreds of clients who soon become abstractions. Thus social workers too often see people with problems not with compassion but as another burden to get rid of as soon as possible. This violation of our people and culture further adds to a sense of despair. Somewhere Latinos have to find stories of transformation and life that are consciously chosen and enacted in the very belly of an impersonal system that reduces all women, Latinas and European-Americans alike, to nonpersons stripped of the capacity to cocreate as selves who relate to each other and to their sacred sources.

THE ARCHETYPE OF THE BATTERED WOMAN

The drama of patriarchy has a number of archetypes that draw their force from this central drama. One of these archetypes that enhances and underpins the story of patriarchy is that of the battered woman.

To physically assault a woman is to practice deformation. The intent is to cripple a woman so that she will not be able to walk away either physically or psychologically. In addition, battering is

intended to disfigure a woman so that she will be repulsive to herself
and unattractive to other men. As a result, abusive men believe that
a woman will have little or no leverage because women under
patriarchy at least had their beauty and, in some cases, their dowry
with which to bargain.

Possessive love together with the drama of patriarchy is a very
formidable obstacle. In Spanish there is a phrase *jaula de oro*, a
golden cage wherein a person is held as a prisoner of love. This
romanticization of the cage does not do justice to the violence of
the entrapment. As we have already seen, the relationship of emanation denies individuality and renders the person to being an
extension of the overwhelming source of mystery of the other. The
mysterious other does not carry this aura owing to any power of
their own; the mystery derives from the underlying archetype that
has a concrete face in one's lover, father, husband, or male guardian.
When the person who is held in emanation ends the relationship,
it is seen as an act of betrayal and so justifies, in the logic of
patriarchy, physical retaliation.

If, on the other hand, the source of emanation withdraws their
approval, the person in emanation becomes suicidal, since their only
purpose for living was the acceptance by the other. Thus possessive
love always lives with the threat of violence owing to its fragility.
As soon as a Latina is tempted in act I, scene 2 to listen to her inner
voice, she can be violently remanded to her place of alleged inferiority. A woman's dreams and desires are considered to be of no
importance. Men exit the core drama in an attempt to restore the
relationship of emanation and thereby practice deformation.

At times the two of these reactions, initiating the break or being
rejected, become combined so that a woman feels disloyal and
suicidal simultaneously. This occurs because she is experiencing
ambivalence; she wants to end the relationship yet, at the same
time, cannot imagine living life without the other. Consequently,
when she is battered, a Latina woman blames herself. She feels that
she deserved the punishment for being disloyal and yet she is relieved
because the assault has put off the burden of creating a new life
and delayed the inevitability of having to enter into the nightmare
of breaking away in act II, scene 1. Thus to be involved in this
drama is to be caught up in a sadomasochistic ritual that turns our
encounters into forms of violence and deformation.

In many cases Latinas refuse to report physical abuse to the authorities because it would constitute a public humiliation of the emanational honor of the family. To be sure, there is also fear because the Latino culture, under the domination of the way of emanation for generations, also legitimized deformation, the submission of women by force. When St. Paul urged women to be submissive to their husbands, it was to become a sacred text that foreshadowed a dark future for Latina women who were left even without recourse to God. There were, and remain, customs in Latin America that allow men to kill their wives for infidelity.

The battering of women is not an issue of class, nor of one's educational level. It is a question of consciousness, and this specific consciousness is given its destructive quality by the way of deformation within which the choice has been made.

Recently I spoke with a young Latina who had been severely beaten by her lover. Both of them are intelligent, university students, attending a prestigious university in the Southwest. During her stay in the hospital, her main concern was her boyfriend. In her mind she felt that she had precipitated the fight and therefore it was her fault. Her first priority was his well-being and not her own. It never crossed her mind to press charges against him. It seems fair to conclude that she had a very poor sense of herself. She had accepted the logic of deformation that threatens women who attempt to reject the drama of patriarchy by killing her own concerns and putting aside her own welfare. In this fashion people participate in their own oppression by accepting complicity in the drama.

During our conversation it was further revealed that she had been abused at home. Her father would strike her and call her names, a form of psychological battering that, in many instances, can be more damaging than physical hurt because of the harm done to one's self-esteem. She always wanted to please her father but no matter how she tried, she could not.

As the discussion continued a further aspect of their combined dramas was uncovered. Her lover, a Latino male, was also routinely beaten by a parent. He hated his life and identified his Latino culture with a sense of shame, poverty, and pain. He was determined to change his life by getting away from home. But as we have seen, removing oneself physically from persons or situations did not free him from the underlying, archetypal drama of patriarchy.

Both the young man and woman were rebelling against their past. By leaving home they felt they had left behind the deformation they had experienced. They realized with a shock that they were repeating the same archetypal dramas that had caused them so much pain. The problem is that both broke only with the inherited, concrete, manifestations of these dramas; what possesses us are the underlying archetypal sources that can only be successfully confronted in act II, scene 2. Since most of us are unaware of these sacred forces in the depths, we are doomed to repeat them. Once again this reinforces how urgent it is to successfully pass through act II, scene 2, by emptying ourselves of the inherited archetypal dramas and to be filled anew with fundamentally more loving and just relationships.

The last time I saw the young woman, she was planning to stay away from her lover in order to reevaluate her life. Still she looked forward to seeing him because she wanted to help him. At the time she was filled with guilt. This is the great poverty of the drama of patriarchy; everybody is crippled. Elaine Pagels has written about the Gospel of St. Thomas. The author of this apocryphal gospel places in the sermons of Jesus the following Gnostic wisdom: "If you discover what is within you, what you discover will save you. If you do not discover what is within you, what you do not discover will destroy you."[14] There is no self, no one is present in possessive love, neither the Latina woman nor the Latino man. Each person loves a projected image but no one is allowed to step forward as a real, vulnerable person. People wear masks, inherited patterns that are intended to cut them off from their deepest sources.

Recently Egyptian writer Naguib Mahfouz's excellent novel, *Palace Walk*, reconfirmed how deeply lost both men and women are in regard to their true selves when they live patriarchal marriages within the way of life of emanation.[15] In addition this work allows us to see the parallels between the political structure of the family and how it is reinforced by the politics of the whole society. Egyptians, prior to the fall of the monarchy under King Farouk, related to the king as the father of the people in the service of emanation. There was no opposition allowed. Ahmad, the father of the family, saw himself as the source of emanation in his own family; he was not to be questioned about anything, especially his right to be with as many women as he chose.

Hence, the two young Latino people mentioned above left home and created a fortress of possessive love that they had hoped could free them from their abusive past. In fact possessive love placed them in a situation to repeat the violent relationships of their respective fathers in the story of patriarchy. Both were in a kind of relationship that deprived them of what they needed most: their creativity, relationships to others, their inner voices, and a new consciousness. The young woman tried but could not really create conflict or change; her attempts to do so ended in a violent confrontation. She became a victim in a way that allowed her to be a martyr. She was willing to continue to risk her well-being if it would help him. This deformational logic is exactly that, logical and true, within the way of deformation. Within this way of life, the self commits suicide, gives oneself over to the other, and suppresses whatever intelligence or insight that might be used to question the relationship.

There is one last aspect to this drama that is disturbing. The Latino community of students was aware of the abuse; the men refused to discuss it or to challenge the young man; the Latinas were angry and wanted to do something about it but got no support from the men. Since the incident, most have tried to forget it or, out of deference to the privacy of the young woman, have dropped the issue. But some realize that it is not just one woman's private problem but a political issue that has historical implications and distorted sacred roots. The dramas and stories of our lives must be told, confronted, and transformed when necessary.

In the way of life of transformation, we love others as we love ourselves. We cannot give ourself to another in love if we hate ourselves or seek to lose our person instead of finding out who we are. The issue here is that we need an alternative perspective, a loving and caring way of life known as transformation that can fill the void of the abyss of violence.

WHERE ARE THE LATINO MEN?

The internal collapse of the Latino family is largely due to the failure of the way of life of emanation. As the family confronts the ways of life of incoherence and deformation, the values instilled in the young are undermined. The previous respect, sense of loyalty, honor, and deference paid to authority and elders is broken. The resulting relationship of incoherence renders the inherited concrete manifestations of the limited repertory of archetypal relationships incapable of dealing with the new changes and conflict. As the young become assimilated in U.S. values in the way of life of incoherence, what catches their attention is the seduction of power. They want what the constant assaults of advertisements promise—wealth and prestige. The old inhibitions based on honor and respect are gone or are at least rapidly dying. The way of life of incoherence looks so promising but most can't make it. Access means schooling more than ever before and, increasingly, technological and scientific training. Many Latino youth have language difficulties in school. So how will they ever make it?

Besides these educational barriers there is the drama of racism as a form of tribalism active in the wider society that increases the dilemma of being successful by the system's own rules. There is no old-boy network established here to get Latinos into the scarce union jobs in the building trades and certainly no network in the banking and corporate realms. To work in a fast-food restaurant earning minimum wage holds no promise for a successful future. This makes the drug culture extremely alluring. Young boys in their teens can make hundreds and even thousands of dollars a week. The new conquering heroes are the drug pushers and their cohorts of bodyguards. Boys are initiated into manhood by experiencing drugs, sex, and gang fights.

Out of the despair that comes from seeing their own fathers often rejected and abused by the wider society and their own experiences of being wounded by the dominant group, many Latino youths turn to forms of self-wounding: drugs, alcohol, and violence. Many drop out of school and become mired in dead-end jobs or turn to crime. This response arises out of a profound depression, out of a feeling of utter powerlessness. They are aware of their victimization at the hands of the powerful. The problem is that the reaction is one that turns the youths into the new victimizers of themselves, their community, and the dominant society. To victimize self and others is not the answer, because this means to practice revenge and to take on the story of the oppressor, the racism inherent in tribalism.

Given this frightening scenario, it is understandable that there is little sense of responsibility to women or the nurturing of children.

Their substitute family is increasingly an emanational relationship
to the members of a gang. So young men are visitors, casual lovers
of the women in the community. Financial responsibility can be
avoided because of the welfare system. Since the couples are so
young there is little to hold them together once the sexual attraction
is over.

Many Latina women have accepted the inevitability of the male
absence and so have bonded among themselves. Social agencies and
community-based organizations become the new extended family,
taking the place of *abuelos* (grandparents) and other family members. The storefront churches, especially the *Pentecostales*, have
been very successful because they often preach a return to a puri-
tanical simplicity of living endowed with the old values. This is
attractive to young women with children and to some young men
who are looking for a firm authoritarian hand, the patriarchal pas-
tor, who will help to put order back into their lives. Often this is
an attempt to revive the way of life of emanation but it cannot
work because the consciousness of emanation as a way of life does
not allow or prepare people to respond to change by creating new
relationships and stories.

In addition, the fiber of the wider society is no longer a container
of shared values but a fragmented, individualistic pursuit of power
in the service of incoherence. As struggles for power proceed, the
rules are constantly shattered so that legal limits become a cynical
joke. With the breakdown of shared rules, there is only naked power
and the rule of the war of all against all, which is exactly what
characterizes the drug culture as the way of life of deformation.

For these reasons, the men are largely "absent" and the situation
promises to deteriorate further. What Latinos must not do is to
accept the sickness that there is nothing that they can do. Latinos
must not end by fulfilling the stereotypes that exist in the stories
of deformation that the powerful have imposed on the Latino community, and which relegate all Latino males to being irresponsible,
prone to dishonesty and immoral living. Many people in the dominant society want to believe this is true by seeing the stereotypes
actualized. Latina women will also have to stop indulging men
because they are so wounded; what Latina women need to do is
challenge men to build fundamentally new and better relationships
with them.

Men and women have to dialogue, to create conflict and change with each other and reject male domination inherent in the story of patriarchy that continues to permeate the Latino culture. The story of patriarchy has to be ended. Women do the bulk of the socializing and nurturing of children. This needs to give way to men accepting a significant and central role in the nurturance of the next generation. Both men and women need to accept the responsibility to adamantly refuse to relate in the socialized, inherited stories of possessive love, patriarchy, matriarchy, and the woman as permanent victim. Latinas and Latinos are not powerless. People have to begin wherever they find themselves in the core drama of transformation to ask themselves what story they are enacting and whether that drama allows them to be whole and loving human beings.

The wider society must also be analyzed and critiqued and changes must be made, especially in regard to ending the racism that continues to do such serious harm to the Latino family and community. It is the wealthy rushing to the suburbs who are largely responsible for substandard education and housing and the flight of the good jobs. This process has to be explained and understood so that whole communities of people stop blaming themselves for the lack of a tax base that leads to the deterioration of all social services. All Latinos, women and men, have to be aggressive in a new way, to step forward urgently to protect the barrio against drugs, redlining by banks, insurance rip-offs, inferior schools, and police brutality.

There is plenty of work to be done by men and women in the personal and political realms so that together they can forge a new history and travel with the god of transformation. As Rosaria said to her husband in the film The Salt of the Earth: "If you do not want the Anglos to dominate you, then neither do we want the men to dominate us."[16] The archetypal way of life of deformation is the same no matter what group weaves it. In the film it is the men and women together who break the hold of the Anglo mine owners and win the union's rightful place to bargain for better wages and living conditions.

CONCLUSION

We now turn to consider in more specific detail the actual breaking of the inherited manifestations of the archetypal relationships, the rejection of the archetypal dramas of patriarchy and possessive love enacted within the ways of life of emanation, incoherence, and deformation in order to plant and nourish alternative stories of life in the service of transformation.

The chapter that follows is based on an archetypal analysis of a Latino couple (Luis and Carmen) that is familiar with the theory of transformation as it has been developed in this book. They are in the process of evaluating their married life as it relates to the ways of life, relationships of dependency, the stories of their lives, and where they currently find themselves in relationship to the core drama of transformation. In addition we will analyze from the perspective of the theory of transformation an extraordinary film, *Lucia*, a story that is fictional but nevertheless authentic because it reveals the patriarchal drama of the family and of male/female relationships in the Latino culture (and others as well). It strikes and resonates a chord within us. The analysis of both the real marriage of Luis and Carmen and the film marriage of Lucia and Tomas, provides us with actual life examples, language and concepts, image and sound that legitimize what many Latinas and Latinos are searching for or are already living.

The struggles of Luis and Carmen, Lucia and Tomas as prototypes of our Latino story dramatize the necessity of doing love and honor to oneself so that we can be empowered to honor and love others as ourselves. Furthermore this real-life story and the film demonstrate the personal, political, historical, and sacred faces of the struggle to create intimate and mutual relationships between men and women. Carmen and Lucia make the choice to courageously destroy the crippling relationship with their husbands. But just as fiercely they refuse to reject or destroy them. This commitment to mutuality radically grounds the core drama of transformation in nonviolence. No one can be commanded to transform; both parties must consciously choose to participate in transforming.

Perhaps the greatest lesson that we can learn from this chapter is how futile it is to be a soft, dependent woman waiting to be fulfilled or complemented by a strong, independent man as was the understanding in the way of life of emanation arrested in act I, scene 1. Both Latina women and Latino men have to be pregnant and to give birth to a self that is both masculine and feminine. Thus in a creative, transforming relationship a man and woman are confirmed in their *wholeness* as a person and *not* as an incomplete man or woman waiting for their opposite to complete them. This is what constitutes act III, scenes 1 and 2 of the core drama of transformation. Yet in another sense wholeness is achieved and our humanity is fulfilled by the other. Thus what Latinos do for each other when they love is discover who they are, each one in their wholeness. Each is given the gift of her or his own self by the other. To be loved is to be affirmed in one's wholeness and to be liberated from possessive love.

NOTES

1. Octavio Paz, "The Sons of La Malinche," in *Introduction to Chicano Studies: A Reader*, Livia Isauro Duran and H. Russell Bernard, eds. (New York: Macmillan, 1973) pp. 22–24.

2. Ibid., pp. 25–27.

3. See Robert S. McIntyre, "The Populist Tax Act of 1989," *The Nation*, April 2, 1988.

4. Frances Fox Piven and Richard A. Cloward, *The New Class War* (New York: Pantheon Books, 1982).

5. *Institute for Puerto Rican Policy*, "Data on the Puerto Rican Community," No. 4 (March 1986).

6. *Report to President Bowen on the Status of Latinos at Princeton University*, Princeton University, May 2, 1985.

7. *The Status of Puerto Ricans in the United States*, published by The National Congress for Puerto Rican Rights, Centro de Estudios Puertoriquenos, Hunter College, City University of New York, May 1987.

8. Direct quote from a talk given at Seton Hall University, March 16, 1988.

9. See "For Children: A Fair Chance, Stop Wasting Lives and Money," *New York Times*, September 6, 1987, editorial page.

10. For an excellent analysis of the more devastating status of the urban underclass see Martha A. Gephart and Robert Pearson, "Contemporary Research on the Urban Underclass," *Items*, 42, no. 12 (June 1988). (*Items* is a publication of the Social Science Research Council, 605 Third Avenue, New York, NY 10158.)

11. John Shockley, *Chicano Revolt in a Texas Town* (Notre Dame, Ind.: University of Notre Dame Press, 1974).

12. I was greatly helped to understand this generational difference among Latinas in a conversation with Ms. Teresita Fernandez-Viña, the director of a community-based organization in the Latino barrio of Chester, Pennsylvania.

13. See Maria E. Perez, *Lo Americano en el Teatro de Sor Juana Ines de la Cruz* (New York: Eliseo Torres and Sons, 1975). Also see Octavio Paz, *Sor Juana*, Margaret Sayers Peden, trans. (Cambridge, Mass.: Harvard University Press, 1988), pp. 100–113.

14. Elaine Pagels, *The Gnostic Gospels* (New York: Random House, 1979), Introduction, p. xv.

15. Naguib Mahfouz, *Palace Walk* (New York: Doubleday, 1990).

16. *Salt of the Earth*, a film directed by Harry Biberman, 1952.

Chapter Five

Latina Female/Latino Male Relationships: Creating New Archetypal Dramas in the Latino Family

In the midst of so much upheaval in the Latino family, we need to read stories of people struggling with their cultural past and an indifferent society for the sake of creating a fundamentally more loving and compassionate present. Because the personal is always also political, historical, and sacred, the stories of Carmen and Luis, whose family we met in Chapter Three, and Lucia and Tomas are not just about two Latino couples; their experiences tell the story of an entire society and culture seeking to give birth to fundamentally new and more loving relationships between men and women. Only relationships enacted within a creative drama of transforming love between men and women will be able to bring forth the kind of Latino family that the times in which we live demand. There is a great need for such stories of transformation as our guides in the midst of so many challenges.

There is a revolution currently taking place in the Latino community that is evident in female/male relationships, especially in the context of the family. It is a revolution not only in the concrete manifestations of male/female relationships but one that is taking place primarily in the depths, in underlying sources. Latinas and Latinos are struggling to cast out, or are at least questioning, their inherited archetypal relationships, dramas, and ways of life in which they have related to each other. Why is this? Many now find their relationships and the stories of their lives to be unbearable and untenable. Let us once again review the theoretical context within which we will reenvision the relationships of men and women as companions and lovers.

As was said earlier, for all of recorded history we have only eight archetypal relationships by which to shape the tensions of everyday life. In the context of this chapter we will concentrate on seeing how the inherited Latino concrete forms of these relationships are actually used and broken, and how new forms of the eight are created in the context of a new story, transforming love, in the service of transformation in act III, scenes 1 and 2. This process will also allow us to see these relationships not as static concepts, categories, or labels that stereotype but as relationships in motion.

As we have seen, all of the sacred dramas or archetypal stories of our lives—such as matriarchy, patriarchy, possessive love, transforming love, tribalism, and the eight archetypal relationships—are practiced in a larger context—the overarching ways of life of emanation, incoherence, deformation, and transformation.[1] I spoke earlier of the fact that there is an underlying revolution taking place so that the struggles Latinos are experiencing in their daily lives are actually concrete manifestations of a deeper contest in their sacred selves.[2] What this means is that daily decisions have a concrete and an underlying archetypal and ultimate significance.

Let us recall that an archetype is the necessary form in which concrete relationships manifest themselves. We experience and enact concrete faces of archetypes at each moment of our lives. Although archetypes are universal, it is essential that individuals give shape to the archetypes in a personal concrete manner.[3] In addition, every archetype is the manifestation of a wider and deeper story, one of the four archetypal ways of life of emanation, incoherence, deformation, or transformation. For this reason it is always necessary when discussing the archetype or idea of love, for example, to ask in the service of what way of life is this love here and now being practiced. This is of utmost importance because love in the service of emanation means the loss of one's identity, whereas love in the service of transformation allows both persons to come forth in their wholeness as individual selves and to create a new and better relationship together that was not there before. Finally, archetypes are the underlying forms that are also sacred. The sacred is a mystery that decisively moves our everyday lives from the depths.

I would like to reiterate four reasons why I use the language of the sacred. First, sacred or religious language has always been part of our Latino heritage; it is a familiar language. However, too often "god" was used in order to legitimize the perpetuation of inherited, concrete manifestations of the eight archetypal relationships and the dramas of life enacted in a particular archetypal way of life. People were made to feel guilt and shame and sin for attempting to break the repertory of relationships that most Latinos were raised with: emanation, subjection, isolation, buffering, and direct exchange in the service of emanation. Thus for generations most Latinos, men and women alike, lived and practiced the inherited, socialized relationships and dramas in the way of life of emanation sanctioned by the society.

Many Latinos are still wrestling with these sacred stories without being able to name them. There are three other reasons to use sacred concepts: the second is that I will be appealing to another understanding of god—that is, to different interpretations of the sacred that will free us to see the sacred in new ways and so that we can respond to the question: Do you believe in god? by responding: No, we don't *believe* in god but we risk *faith* in god by determining in the service of what way of life this god inspires us. Third, I am not interested in restoring any kind of lost orthodoxy or a return to the one, true, everlasting truth. Finally, the language of the sacred allows us to explain where the fundamentally new has it origins in our lives.[4]

Our understanding of different archetypal ways of life that are inspired by different sacred sources or gods allows us to reject a god if that god is in fact the lord of emanation, incoherence, or deformation. This frees us to choose to respond to the invitation of the lord of transformation as our guide escorting us through the core drama of transformation again and again. In this way we do not have to deny the sacred or god; it is specific gods that we can now name that wound us, because they can only inspire us to be partial selves in the service of the ways of life of emanation, incoherence, and deformation.

In the midst of the struggle to live meaningful lives, all of us are actually inspired by different underlying sacred sources to make

choices that have personal, political, historical, and sacred implications. This means that there are competing archetypal dramas
and ways of life and sacred sources that are *in-spiring*, or breathing
within us. This gives us as human beings the opportunity to distinguish between these lords and to choose the lord of transformation,
the only god with whom we can participate in creating fundamentally more loving and fulfilling families.

LA FAMILIA LATINA: CHOOSING BETWEEN
WAYS OF LIFE AND DEATH

As we have seen, the story of the family usually enacted in the
way of life of emanation by Latinos is patriarchy.[5] This means that
for generations Latina women and Latino men remained objects
who were shaped by the past rather than asserting themselves as
subjects who could act upon and create history.

Politically, people remained uncritically loyal regardless of their
wealth or poverty because the ruler as father was linked to God
the Father in a chain of emanational links that connected the authority of the sacred and the state to the father of the family. The
underlying source that guaranteed this way of life was the god of
emanation, who granted a total security for the society by providing
legitimacy and an ultimate unity to this web of life. All of life had
meaning that was ultimately mysterious and all knew who they
were in this given state of enchantment.

It is my contention that the way of life of emanation was the way
of life within which most archetypal dramas of female/male Latino
relationships were lived for centuries. In addition, all of the eight
relationships to be further described in creating and telling new
sacred dramas or stories were usually limited to a repertory of five
relationships. Latina women practiced relationships of dependency
that, if skillfully practiced, at times allowed some women to dominate men through covert manipulation. It was a power struggle
but a struggle within a way of life that crippled both men and
women for reasons that will be developed.[6]

It is important to stress once again that this theory does not allow
us to stereotype. All four ultimate ways were always available to
individuals and to the entire Latino community. For this reason I
do not equate premodern times with the way of life of emanation

or even use the term "traditional." It was always possible for Latinos to break with an inherited archetypal drama, with a socialized repertory of relationships and way of life and to enact something radically different. Since the beginning there were Latino people, men and women in their families, who practiced dramas in the service of transformation that put them at odds with their society.

Our task in this book is not only to do empirical analysis but to go beyond the concrete facts in order to determine the quality of life that was being lived. To determine the quality of life is the task and benefit of archetypal analysis. Therefore, we must ever ask anew what way of life is involved, what drama is being played out, who are the actors on stage, what aspects of their personalities are being enacted, which relationships are they forbidden to use? This means to view the cosmos of human relations as in a process of continuous creation.

RELATIONSHIPS OF DEPENDENCY IN THE SERVICE OF EMANATION

The specific, inherited manifestations of the eight archetypal relations that were legitimately practiced by Latina women living within the way of life of emanation were limited to a repertory of five relationships: emanation, subjection, isolation (psychological), buffering, and direct exchange. The other three relationships of boundary management, incoherence, and transformation were forbidden because they were rightfully seen as a threat to the web of life guaranteed by the way of life of emanation. However, what must be stressed once more is that the eight archetypal relationships are neither negative nor positive in themselves; as we have seen, relationships and the stories of our life draw their deeper meaning from the ultimate way of life in which we live our lives.

But ways of life are vulnerable. Emanation as a way of life inspired by sacred, underlying sources is shaken to the roots when it can no longer convince its followers that suffering and misfortune are the inevitable will of god; when it can no longer provide total security and when it cannot cope with new problems that create profound doubts, then the network of life begins to fragment.

When this crumbling of the foundations takes place, people can try to unconsciously repress their doubts by renewing their loyalty to this way of life. Or they can consciously suppress their new insights. But given the choices revealed by the theory of transformation, it is possible to see this breaking of a way of life as the call from the deepest depths in scene 2 of act I to begin a dangerous but necessary journey toward wholeness and transformation. It is necessary to "sin," to rebel, to polarize, to violate the codes of the legitimate society, to break with those individuals and institutions that hold life together, in order to enter act II, scene 1.

Many Latinos experience the painful incoherence of living between two ways of life, the powerfully charged emanational fragments carried by our parents to the *barrios* of this country and the demands of this society that they be competitive, aggressive, and possessive individualists. This *choque de las culturas* (clash of cultures) was at times made more painful by parents who were masters of guilt (*remordimiento*) and who were always there to threaten that failures were a *castigo de Dios* (punishment from God). Many did not want to assimilate but they also knew that they couldn't live an emanational past. Entering into act II, scene 1, breaking with the container of emanation, is a frightening but a necessary step in the archetypal structure of the journey of transformation.

THE CORE DRAMA OF TRANSFORMATION:
FEMALE/MALE LATINO RELATIONSHIPS

All of us begin at the very least in the *relationship* of emanation, a connection in which we are extensions of a mysterious source that we cannot understand. Increasingly this relationship of emanation is a substitute for the whole way of life of emanation that is now everywhere being questioned and dying. All of us need to begin and, indeed according to the very nature of creation, come forth as emanations of the sacred, our parents, and given world. But the relationship of emanation is ever more important because Latinos are increasingly living in the world of incoherence where all of their inherited, concrete manifestations of the eight archetypal relationships are breaking. Since the way of life of emanation is dying, they hang onto fragments of this way of life, especially the relationship of emanation, which allows them to have a safe haven.[7]

However, to achieve wholeness, and to participate in shaping the society around them, Latinos must come forth and not arrest their lives in this relationship. In breaking with the person with whom one was previously linked in emanation, one enters into act II, scene 1 or the relationship of incoherence. Incoherence as a relationship is the experience of standing in the presence of a person with whom we were previously linked in emanation and not knowing how to relate. This is both negative and positive; it is negative because a sense of self-identity forged in security to mysterious others in now gone; it is positive because now a Latina woman can begin to live the inherent structure of her life, which is to practice the craft of the alchemists who dissolved base metals and experimented with this process until they discovered a deeper mystery in the melting and recoagulation of materials: an analogy of the finding of the self.[8]

Act II, scene 2 is the turning point in the core drama of transformation. If a Latina succeeds only in breaking with her actual lover in act II, scene 1, unless she also leaves behind the archetypal drama of patriarchy in act II, scene 2, she will repeat the same drama by enacting only a concrete substitution, one lover replaces another. Thus she achieves only reformation not transformation in the way of life of emanation. This kind of reformation means that the god of emanation is able to raise up new lovers for Latinas who will provide the security that the other failed to do. The reformation ends by a woman making herself into what the male wants her to be. She has reformed but not transformed, defined by the same god, in the same way of life, repeating the same archetypal drama of security in a patriarchal embrace.

Therefore what is necessary is to say no three times over: not only to the actual jealous lover in act II, scene 1, but also in act II, scene 2 to the sacred story of patriarchy enacted in the way of life of emanation. We are very vulnerable in this condition; we are actually wounded owing to the vacuum caused by the broken connections with mysterious others. But the sacred source or god of the way of life of emanation is also wounded and seeks to restore the torn web of emanation by having Latina women return even more docilely to this way of life. To persist in saying no is to reject the in-spiring of this lord. Yet Latinas are still waiting to be filled anew and there are competing sacred sources who seek to heal them according to their grace. At this point, the god of the way of incoherence can speak within and say that there is no other way to

survive except by gaining power and building a fortress within
which to protect a wounded self.

The Way of Life of Incoherence

The relationship of incoherence, breaking away from others, as
seen earlier, was intended to be only a step (act II, scene 1) in the
process toward transformation. However, by remaining permanently polarized and angry, the relationship of incoherence is turned
into the whole way of life of incoherence. The journey is arrested
and people become permanently rebellious adolescents in act II,
scene 1. What began as a step toward wholeness now becomes the
whole overarching way of life of incoherence. In this way of life,
there is no ultimate meaning, love, truth, or beauty. This is the
dominant way of life that surrounds *la familia Latina* in current
U.S. society.[9] Latinos feel forced to protect themselves by pursuing
self-interest and power. Our personal face is consciously suppressed
because in this way of life no one can afford intimacy, closeness to
self or others; the political is reduced to power politics, acquiring
power or attaching oneself to powerful others; history becomes the
realm of the powerful who pursue power in order to become ever
more powerful fragments in a world of fragmented people; history,
therefore, becomes a persistent competition among fragments.

Our sacred face in this way of life is hidden, repressed, and,
therefore, is much more dangerous; it does not go away but remains
to inspire Latinos to say that this is the only way reality can be,
that life is unfair and that one must accept the brutality of life. So
in this official way of life of U.S. society, Latinos settle for less and
learn to live with incoherence, which is really to limit themselves
to accept organized insecurity.[10] Why is this? Because Latinos increasingly no longer share common values, ideals, and authority
patterns, as they did in the way of life of emanation, they feel freed
from these constraints so that a neighbor is now a potential threat
and enemy. They feel they have no choice but to live a life of
calculated self-interest that is always insecure because everyone is
forced to look over their shoulder. This is really the dominant liberal
way of life and the story of the market society that is being described.
For this reason, many Latinos have always been opposed to assimilation into the dominant culture. To assimilate is actually to become

like the others with power and in so doing repress or suppress their sense of love, truth, beauty, and community.

Now Latinos enact a limited repertory of concrete manifestations of the eight archetypal relationships. However, these relationships are enacted in the service of incoherence, particularly boundary management, direct exchange, isolation, and subjection. Latinos now use whatever relationships the powerful allow them to exercise.

Latinos caught in this stunted way of life are immobilized because they cannot use their awareness of the organized insecurity that characterizes the scramble in the way of life of incoherence to go beyond it. Because they are dominated by the logic of this way of life, they cannot see the possibility of something fundamentally new and better, only the fear of something worse.

The Way of Life of Deformation

However, incoherence is also vulnerable as a way of life.[11] Incoherence as a way of life becomes unbearable when its methods of organizing anxiety become fruitless. Incoherence as a whole way of life opens another deeper danger—that of deformation. Because nobody knows or cares about people in their wholeness as persons but rather as social security numbers, they may look to a gang, a substance, a hero, a political leader, a religious movement to remove them from the perpetual anxiety of having no power to survive in a hostile society. In these conditions people clutch onto a fragment of life, such as being the member of a gang, that provides them with powerful symbols of security and identity in the group. Only the group is valid; outsiders are the enemy.

This is really a pseudo container or fake way of life of emanation because it promises a return to a golden age that never really existed. The way of life of deformation plunges us deeper into despair because it is based on a lie, a fragment of life, such as gender, ethnicity, skin color, or religion, turned into a fantasy, into a whole way of inflicting death on black and brown people, on women, gays, on a religious group, or even on members of one's own community who have become expendable. Thus, by turning maleness, race, ethnicity, drug profits, or one's religion into a whole way of life, the humanity of the outsider is denied. This is truly the realm of Satan, of no exit, of the lord of nothing. Here reformation is fully corrupted to become something fundamentally new but worse, the way of life of deformation.[12]

In order to prevent polarizing the relationship of incoherence from becoming the way of life of incoherence or descending into the abyss of the way of deformation, the pain experienced in act II, scene 1 must be allowed to lead to a critical consciousness that the way of life of emanation is unbearable and to which it is impossible to return; furthermore, that the way of life of incoherence is unfruitful in its brutal pursuit of power; and that the way of life of deformation is a descent into madness. We are blessed to have another sacred guide, the god of transformation, by whom we are guided as participants into the ceremony of act II, scene 2, wherein we free ourselves of the lord, the story that possesses our soul, and prepare to meet the sacred in a more loving and compassionate way in act III, scenes 1 and 2.

The Way of Life of Transformation: Male/Female Relationships

The way of life of transformation is the only real alternative for Latinos as they confront the other incomplete and frustrated ways of life. Emanation, incoherence, and deformation are all failed and truncated versions of the way of life of transformation. In the way of life of transformation, all are inspired to see themselves as participants, as guides of transformation who are persistent creators together with the source of sources of the world. Now all eight archetypal relationships, all archetypes, and all archetypal dramas can be reconstituted and practiced and new archetypes created in the overarching way of life of transformation.

Latinos can now begin by creating new concrete forms of the eight archetypal relationships. In the service of transformation Latinos are no longer permanently caught by the inherited forms of the relationships; they are free to use all eight of the relationships in a temporary manner so that there is the ability to respond to new problems. For example, the relationship of emanation in the way of life of transformation is the experience of security where we always begin in the merciful embrace of those who love us. But Latinos must distance themselves through struggle from those who necessarily begin as the source of their mystery by listening to their inner voice in act I, scene 2 and sever connections in act II, scene 1 so that they can understand, distinguish between, and, above all, make choices among the sources that are involved and what they are asking of them; but then they must go beyond this philosophical stance by becoming true practitioners of transformation.

For this reason Latinos must also enter act II, scene 2 and empty themselves of the sacred sources that gave their stories their mysterious hold over them. In act III, scenes 1 and 2, their personal lives now emerge and they consciously seek to practice strategies of transformation; they are now free to create, nourish, destroy, and re-create an infinite number of new manifestations of the eight archetypal relationships and choose among or create new archetypal dramas to be enacted within the ultimate way of life of transformation.

Politically, a Latina is now free to shape her environment to treat each person as sacred; what she can and needs to do together with others as a citizen of the polis is to exercise her capacity to deal afresh with every new problem in the way of life of transformation. Historically, she is no longer a passive receiver of the past, but she becomes an active subject who can shape new turning points in the spiral of history toward the fundamentally new and better.

Our sacred guide, the god of transformation, now makes it possible for Latinas to draw upon their deepest sources: they and the sacred are transforming. In regard to the particular problem, that of the story of patriarchy, to be dealt with in this chapter, Latinas and Latinos can now be inspired to realize that they can create *mutual* love between men and women, not power relationships, but mutual vulnerability so that they heal the wounds and release the repressed energies within. And finally, in act III, scene 2 they become whole, not perfect, finished, or model citizens, but whole in the sense that in regard to this specific problem they have enacted a new and better story, the drama of transforming love. All of this process is, however, never final. It is a testimony, an act of faith in the future that if Latinos have successfully found wholeness in one realm of their lives they can practice this kind of transformation again and again in all aspects of their lives in regard to any and all problems.

Male/female Latino relationships are not, therefore, a sideshow of the political change in the public realm; the personal is also political, historical, and sacred. Thus the real revolution is taking place both in concrete relationships and in the underlying sources of Latina women and Latino men. The struggle between men and women holds the key to creating a more human family. When a Latina woman rebels and thereby enters into act II, scene 1, she is not just shaking her fist at one particular male with whom she was previously linked in the relationship of emanation in act I, scene 1, but she is also rejecting the political and historical legitimacy of the archetypal drama of patriarchy that for generations institutionalized its frozen relationships of dependency as the will of god by which society gave men the right to dominate women. For this reason a Latina woman also enters act II, scene 2 wherein she empties herself of the story that possessed her life.

In addition, she dissents from the whole way of life of emanation jealously guarded by a sacred source, the god of emanation, that gives authority to patriarchal religion. Thus, the personal interpenetrates with the political, historical, and sacred faces of her being. Now Latina women are ready on the edge of this new history to be filled anew by the spirit in act III, scenes 1 and 2.

What is badly needed are examples drawn from one's own experience and the best of Latino contemporary artists who produce novels, stories, plays, poetry, films, philosophy, psychology, and theology as guides for us so that the potential revolution does not become a sterile rebellion by returning to a more powerful container, (in the way of life of emanation), deciding to live with suppression and settling for less (the way of life of incoherence) or worse, falling into deformation (resorting to violence to attempt to restore the old).

Why make use of films and literature that are works of fiction? They touch us all deeply precisely because we see dramatized in the lives of the characters or the focused emotion of the poet the very archetypal dramas, relationships, and ways of life that the Latino family is at present confronting. In other words, they tell the story of Latinas and Latinos in the daily encounters of life.

LUCIA: COMPETING ARCHETYPAL DRAMAS AND WAYS OF LIFE

To understand the new archetypal dramas and ways of life that are at stake in the struggle of the Latino family, I will analyze a

Cuban film, *Lucia*.[13] We will use this work of revolutionary art to create a dialectic with the theory of transformation so we can see whether or not the underlying structure of life is indeed refracted through a theoretical lens that promises us both theory and practice, the normative and the empirical.

Lucia is a 1968 Cuban film directed by Humberto Solas. It deals with male/female relationships in three periods of Cuban history: the revolt against Spain in 1895, the dictatorship of Gerardo Machado in 1932, and the Cuban Revolution in 196–. The final period of the film, the Cuban Revolution, is deliberately dated 196– with no final digit in order to point out the nature of revolution—that it must be ongoing, a permanent process of transformation. This latter historical stage of the Cuban Revolution as covered in the film will be the focus of our analysis.

I had promised earlier to point out examples of inherited concrete manifestations of the eight archetypal relationships, emerging archetypal dramas, and the competing ways of life and their sacred underlying sources that inspire these ways of life. In the relationship between Lucia and Tomas in the film we can clearly see the struggle between the forbidden and the acceptable ways of life, dramas, and relationships by closely observing the dialogue.

The relationships of dependence of Cuban/Latina women are evident in the statements in Figure 3 (which will be used to give concrete examples of the eight archetypal relationships and ways of life spoken of above, together with symbols that represent these archetypal sources, originally described in Figure 2).

Initially, when we meet Lucia in the third phase of the film, 196–, she is working with a brigade of women and is very happy. She feels good about herself; she is a productive worker and she is in love. It is clear that the director, Humberto Solas, is making a positive statement about the role of government, of the Cuban Revolution, in helping women to become equal members of society. Yet, Tomas is too simply caricatured as the regressive, backsliding, macho husband still mired in the past. Nevertheless, Tomas represents the fundamental difference between the change of behavior modification inherent in reformation and the underlying revolution of transformation.

Any government can declare a revolution to be in place and provide punishment or incentives such as better housing to those

Figure 3
Eight Archetypal Relationships and Four Archetypical Ways of Life:
Applying Theory to Practice

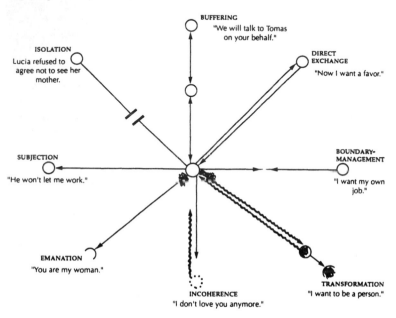

BUFFERING
"We will talk to Tomas on your behalf."

ISOLATION
Lucia refused to agree not to see her mother.

DIRECT EXCHANGE
"Now I want a favor."

SUBJECTION
"He won't let me work."

BOUNDARY-MANAGEMENT
"I want my own job."

EMANATION
"You are my woman."

INCOHERENCE
"I don't love you anymore."

TRANSFORMATION
"I want to be a person."

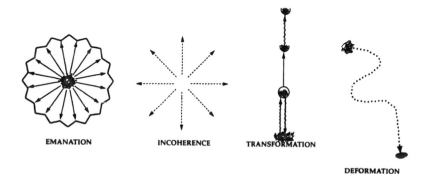

EMANATION

INCOHERENCE

TRANSFORMATION

DEFORMATION

families in which both husband and wife work. But if this is merely external, social adaptation in order to achieve benefits, then the same archetypal drama of patriarchy will surface again because no transformation has taken place in the depths; the people have not *chosen* the revolution, only the rhetoric and the subjection of the revolution. So Tomas is not simply a reactionary; he represents a much more complicated person who wants to be a good revolutionary; but when it comes to his wife, he cannot find his way. Transformation or revolution take place only in individuals who, along with others, consciously choose to change their society for the better by emptying themselves on the deeper level of inherited archetypal dramas that strangle their humanity. Tomas has to go through the journey of transformation in relationship to a particular problem—his relationship to his wife in the context of the inherited understanding of the Latino family.

From Figure 3 we can see that in the beginning of their marriage Tomas relates to Lucia in the drama of patriarchy with a limited repertory of four relationships, in the service of emanation, in act I, scene 1 of the core drama. Let us now reconsider these concrete, inherited manifestations of four of the eight archetypal relationships from the vantage point of this film.

Emanation is a relationship in which you or I are extensions of a mysterious other who determines the changes and conflicts for us but who demands unyielding loyalty of ourselves in continuous cooperation with their decisions. The justice of such enchantment is security; the cost is one's own selfhood: "Lo que pasa es que tu eres mi mujer; vas a ser para mi nomas" (What is involved here is that you are my woman; you belong only to me).

In the relationship of subjection Lucia is no longer being denied a separate existence but now she very clearly knows that the source of her fear is retaliation by Tomas if she dares to threaten his authority. Lucia cannot create conflict or change and is committed to continue to collaborate with Tomas in order to survive. "Dice que no puedo trabajar." "En mi casa mando yo" (He says I cannot work. In my house I am the boss), shouts Tomas.

In the relationship of buffering, Lucia seeks respite from the unyielding tension of emanation and subjection. She looks to a third party, her former co-workers, to intervene in order to improve her situation by creating conflict and change on her behalf so as to be

able to gain a better deal from the powerful other: "Nosotros hab-
lamos con el" (We shall speak to him) Lucia is assured by her
friends. In direct exchange, Lucia attempts to achieve conflict and
change through her own efforts; she speaks up to Tomas and asks
for a favor that will help her to remain loyal to him. She sees her
chance as Tomas becomes affectionate and sexually playful. Lucia,
as do the women in all patriarchal societies, has to use covert
manipulation to achieve changes: "Oye yo quiero una cosa. Que
cosa? Quiero ver a mi mama" (I would like a favor. What is it? I
want to see my mother). But Tomas is not interested in loosening
the tension of the relationships of emanation and subjection by even
allowing buffering and direct exchange.

These two latter relationships actually provide the elasticity, the
steam valve for the dominant relationships of emanation and subjection; these two relationships of buffering and direct exchange
are intended to head off real changes—that is, prevent the forbidden
relationship of incoherence, the breaking of connections, by reducing the anger of the woman to a commodity that will purchase
some benefits only so she will become even more loyal and obedient
and therefore return to "normal," the relationship of emanation.
Tomas refuses to allow Lucia to see her mother except when he is
home because he fears a meddling mother-in-law who might act as
a buffer to put ideas in her daughter's head.

Tomas pushes Lucia back into the relationships of emanation
and subjection by telling her all the men are drooling over her and
"el unico que come soy yo" (the only one who will enjoy you is
me). This statement with stark brutality expresses the total loss of
a woman's identity in the story of patriarchy practiced in the way
of life of emanation in act I, scene 1. Tomas actually means that
Lucia is his to devour as he pleases. In addition, there will be no
further discussion of the issue: "Bueno, me dejas ir? Tu sabes que
yo solo tengo una palabra" (Well, can I go? You know that I have
already made up my mind). The door of subjection closes the attempt to bargain thus pushing Lucia toward rebellion.

Isolation is a relationship in which two people *mutually* agree to
leave each other alone; they thus cooperate in avoiding any conflict
or change in order to continue the relationship. This relationship
is *psychologically* available to Lucia and, historically, to Latina
women—that is, Latinas were allowed to withdraw into themselves,

into a moody silence or pensive state but they were not *physically* allowed to leave for any extended period of time without permission. Tomas does not allow Lucia to leave the house at all while he is away, "Ni la deja parar en la puerta" (He won't even let her stand in the doorway), as the neighbors observe. And, of course, he will not allow her to work because of his fear that this will allow her to become independent of him by practicing the relationship of boundary management. But even psychological isolation was denied Lucia. In one specific scene Lucia is moody and Tomas is offended by her silence and so he attempts to draw out her thoughts so that he can deflect the reason for her psychological withdrawal: her unhappiness of not being able to work or go out.

FORBIDDEN RELATIONSHIPS

The encounter of boundary management is a forbidden relationship in patriarchal societies, which the Cuban Revolution had actually legitimized for Cuban women like Lucia. When we first meet Lucia she is happy working with a whole brigade of women. Women were given the right by the Cuban Revolution to exercise autonomy, which on the personal level allows independence for the self. An individual can accrue skills and an area of competence that allows them to establish economic independence. But the relationship of boundary management also carries a potentially revolutionary aspect. Autonomy on the group level makes it possible for people to organize together around a common issue and to sustain each other over a period of time in pursuit of specific goals. For the first time boundary management can be created to empower marginal people. This actually involves polarization because the previously excluded can now participate in a new venture on the basis of shared new principles as against the principles of established political power that excluded them.

When Tomas married Lucia he immediately forbade her to work because he intuited that her autonomy was a threat to his idea of a docile, dependent woman who should be happy staying at home. In fact, Tomas was more rigid than the culture allowed because, as we have seen, he did not allow even buffering or direct exchange or psychological isolation to ease the harshness of emanation and subjection. In the film, Tomas is told by Flavio, the local Communist leader, that if he allowed his wife to work it would be beneficial because the government was giving preference for better housing to couples that worked. In this way, the government was decisively intervening to break inherited male/female relationships by acting as a buffering agent and bargaining for this change by offering housing benefits. Tomas quickly rejected these interventions by the government. As a matter of fact, Lucia tells us that Tomas had told her: "que el [Tomas] es la revolución" (that he [Tomas] is the revolution). In other words, he, Tomas, is the source of the mystery, to whom Lucia should dedicate herself. Of course this is a stereotypical counterrevolutionary statement.

But this is more than the use of humor to veil state propaganda on behalf of the Cuban government. I believe that hidden within this statement was a subtle criticism by the director, Solas, not only of Tomas but of all males, including Castro and other leaders, that the revolution is greater than the whims of the male military clique. In addition, there is another underlying danger here. If the revolution succeeded in breaking the emanational hold of men over women, there was a danger that the intent was merely to transfer the loyalty of the women from the men to the revolutionary state as the new source of overwhelming mystery that was to be uncritically accepted.[14] If this were to happen we would have a reformation, not a transformation, in the way of life of emanation. Women would indeed be changing but rather than being who they choose to be they would be creating themselves in the image of what the government saw as desirable.[15] This is one of the strengths of our theory; it does not allow us to pronounce a revolution, family, or marriage as transformed, once and for all. We have to continue to see which relationships are present, which are forbidden, which archetypal drama is involved, which way of life is being chosen, and which sacred source is inspiring us in regard to this particular problem.

Incoherence is a relationship in which two persons stand in the presence of each other and cannot agree on how to relate. The inherited repertory of only five of the eight archetypal relationships enacted in the way of life of emanation that shaped male/female Latino relationships is breaking; everything is conflict and change, there is no continuity or cooperation and also no justice for either. When Lucia was told she could not work and therefore gave up

her initial enjoyment of autonomy, she turned to fantasy, sexual
play, and teasing her husband as buffers to hide her growing incoherence. Through a series of maneuvers, Tomas makes Lucia feel
guilty, vulnerable, or ungrateful and so is able to seduce her to
return loyally to her duty as faithful wife. To watch films like this
and to see the eight relationships in motion helps us to realize that
life enacted in the service of emanation was never static yet increasingly unworkable and unbearable. Tomas and Lucia are constantly
dealing with Tomas's insecurity as he strives to be the source of
her mystery in emanation, dominates her in subjection if she shows
disrespect, refuses to allow buffers or her sexual bargaining to
loosen the reins of control.

What is at stake in all of these encounters is a whole way of life,
that of emanation, which in its personal, political, historical, and
sacred aspects is dying. Musical lyrics throughout the film tell us
that the woman is no longer the slave of the man and that times
have changed. Yet on the deeper level where revolutions are truly
at stake, Tomas is still dominated by the archetypal story of the
patriarchy that is a story in the service of the dying way of life of
emanation. Lucia and Tomas both *know* intellectually at least, due
to the rhetoric of the revolution, that this way is actively discouraged, and that the container for both has begun to break. Tomas
has to spend more and more energy rebuilding Lucia's belief in his
manhood as her emanational source of security.

Slowly Lucia's doubts increasingly turn the repression of act I,
scene 1 into scene 2; Lucia is listening to her own inner desires.
Still Lucia is reluctant to enter into act II, scene 1, the relationship
of incoherence, actually rupturing her relationship with Tomas. At
one point she says to her male teacher, sent from Havana as part
of a literacy campaign: "Bueno, es mi marido. Pero que es lo que
tu quieres que yo haga? Ademas yo lo quiero asi" (Well, after all
he is my husband. What is it that you want me to do? In any case
this is the way I want him to be). These statements are rationali-
zations or buffers hiding her deep unhappiness.

As long as Lucia represses the pain and doubt of her inner conflicts
in act I, scene 2, it cannot become critical consciousness and therefore a step on the way toward transformation. Transformation is
forbidden and impossible in this context because Lucia refuses to
admit the problem. She is crippled and cut off from her deepest

sources and so cannot exercise new consciousness, creativity, new linkages to others, or a shared justice. This really means that Lucia, at this point in the story, does not see herself as a person capable of entering into rebellion in act II, scene 1, and of freeing herself from destructive dramas in act II, scene 2. Because of this she deprives herself of the possibility of transformation.

Transformation is a way of life in which all eight relationships are rediscovered and reconstituted so that they are not mere repeats of the past. Lucia is tempted not to create anything new, but to return to the past. Rather than creating fundamentally new and better relationships in the service of transformation, a false consciousness can lead one to reform oneself by turning into a more intensely loyal disciple in the way of life of emanation, or into a more powerful person who rejects all love and vulnerability in the way of life of incoherence, or, in the abyss, change becomes deformation—the creation of the fundamentally new but worse when one or both persons turn to violence against self or other.

The teacher from Havana becomes Lucia's guide who breaks through her protestations and buffers to tell her: "Lucia, la mujer no es esclava de su marido" (Lucia, a woman is not her husband's slave). Lucia, with this encouragement, this time successfully creates incoherence and enters into act II, scene 1; Lucia runs away from Tomas. Earlier her requests to go back to work, to go out in public, and to end her dependence were actually efforts to exercise the forbidden relationships of boundary management and physical isolation in a patriarchal marriage. These attempts, which threatened the marriage, were rendered useless by Tomas's use of the relationship of subjection in the service of emanation. In the film we are also told that Tomas's father had done the same to his wife, "clipped her wings." This comment is important because it demonstrates how all of us will simply repeat the archetypal dramas and ways of life and will worship the gods of our body politic and society until a person or group consciously decides to break the established ways of relating and thereby create incoherence.

Because Tomas still lives enchanted and enchained in the way of emanation, a truncated and fragile way of life, he is not capable, given the logic of this once-and-for-all world, to let Lucia go or to transform his own behavior. Thus Tomas turns to violence to forcefully attempt to put together his collapsing way of life. The relationship of subjection, which had been acceptable in the way of life of emanation as long as Lucia and Latina women believed in the fundamental justice of this way of life, now becomes normless violence. For Lucia what Tomas is doing no longer holds legitimacy. Thus, his use of subjection does not return her to "normal"—that is, back to docile loyalty in act I, scene 1. Lucia is now so angry that she enters into open defiance in act II, scene 1 of the core drama.

THE RELATIONSHIP OF INCOHERENCE IN THE SERVICE OF TRANSFORMATION

Lucia's incoherence, leaving Tomas and entering into act II, scene 1, is now leading her to true revolution; it is not used as a bargaining ploy to get a better deal within the existing system of patriarchal marriage and family but it is a revolutionary act of rejecting *all* the old inherited relationships legitimized by generations of male authority within the archetypal drama of patriarchy, the way of life of emanation, as well as a conscious refusal to allow Tomas to beat her and thus practice the way of deformation. All of these stories, together with the gods that energize and legitimize these ways of life, are rejected. Lucia's teacher urges her to make the break: "No lo pienses mal, Lucia. Vete. Es que yo tengo miedo y ademas yo lo quiero" (Don't think that you are doing something wrong. Go. But I am afraid, and besides, I love him). Tomas hears the advice being given and a fight breaks out with the teacher. For Lucia this is the end of the marriage. She leaves a note: "I am going. I am not a slave." These are the first words that Lucia has ever written. For Lucia literacy is really a transforming act of liberation. In finding her own voice and desires, Lucia is firmly rooted in her own authenticity.

It is important to note here that Lucia's personal emergence is also political, because she is not only resisting one man, Tomas, but the cultural and social structures that gave men the right to control her life. This is a turning point in Lucia's life as well as the lives of other women who can now realize that history is not a condemnation to live in endless cycles of deadly repetition; the life of each woman is valuable and therefore sacred. In this way Lucia has dramatically changed the four faces of her being.

At this point Tomas's patriarchal world, arrested in act I, scene 1 of the core drama, is crumbling. He gets drunk, goes home, and sees that Lucia is gone; he is absent from work and cannot function. This experience of incoherence for Tomas, as often happens to the previously powerful, moves him into deformation. He now seeks out Lucia, intent on returning her through violence to a marriage, and to a male/female relationship enacted in the drama of patriarchy. But he cannot promise either of them the old security of the dying way of life of emanation. So rather than attempt to create new and better connections, his inspiration is to use violence justified by a fragment of life, invested with the illusion of being the whole meaning of life, his wounded pride as a patriarchal male and husband.

For Lucia to have returned at this point of her journey would have been a murder of the self,[16] because she has become fully awakened to who she is and can become. This would have been no return but an exit from the core drama and the acceptance of an abysmal life. This would be deformation because Lucia would have to consciously deny who she is and accept a way of destructive death, not only for herself but also for Tomas and, symbolically and politically, for all women. Furthermore, she would have accepted and enhanced Tomas's attempt to turn his injured masculinity into a whole fantasy dominating their lives for the worse in the way of deformation.

Tomas tries to force Lucia to come back home. She tells him clearly, "Ya no te quiero" (I don't love you anymore). Tomas insists, "Yo soy tu marido" (I am your husband). But it is clear that Lucia has broken with Tomas and has created the relationship of incoherence and entered into act II, scene 1. Now the greatest risk arises for Lucia. She truly loves Tomas; she can't eat and is very unhappy. Tomas is in a similar condition. The power of sacred stories such as patriarchy is so strong that they continue to enchant us and to whisper in our ears that the only answer is to go back. Tomas is not the problem at this point in the core drama; it is the story that possesses both Lucia and Tomas. Unless Lucia sustains her journey and successfully enters into act II, scene 2 of the core drama and empties herself, not only of Tomas but of the story of patriarchy and the way of life of emanation that inspired the story, she will repeat the drama either with Tomas or with another man.

The risk is that Lucia will abort the journey by using their separation as a bargaining tool or perhaps to revenge herself on Tomas. Lucia goes looking for Tomas and he is ecstatic to see her return and assumes that she has given in to his wishes: "I knew that you would change because I love you so much." But Lucia answers that he has to let her work. Tomas tells Lucia to get away from him. She refuses: "Yo voy a seguir contigo. No me voy" (I am going to stay with you. I am not going). Tomas becomes violent and Lucia says, "Not like that, not like that" (Asi, no. Asi, no). "Or I am not going to love you any more" (O te voy a dejar de querer). Lucia cannot go back to the old: "Yo tengo que servir para algo. Pero yo no puedo seguir como antes. Yo voy a seguir trabajando y tu me vas a dejar vivir" (I have to be somebody. I can't go on living as I did before. I am going to continue working and you are going to let me live).

Tomas is suffering from the consciousness of the story of patriarchy enacted in the way of life of emanation and, when he becomes violent, in the service of deformation. He continues to live in a male world that severely limits and indeed makes impossible a new relationship with a woman who is radically new and better. Lucia does not want to leave or divorce Tomas; she is not interested in hurting him and thereby seeking revenge in the service of deformation. Nor does Lucia seek to go back to a marriage in the way of life of emanation; for Lucia her marriage to Tomas in the story of patriarchy in the service of emanation is gone for good.

What Lucia wants is to have a marriage with Tomas, not a marriage that possesses them. Lucia is really trying to create a new marriage that will allow both of them to come forth as whole human beings. However, Tomas assumed that because Lucia loved him and sought him out that she had given in to the inherited, concrete manifestations of the relationships of dependence found in the drama of patriarchy in the service of emanation. In short, that she had realized her mistake and was returning to be a good wife. However, Lucia wants to participate in a truly imaginative revolution by emptying herself in act II, scene 2 of the story of patriarchy; she wants to forge a new archetypal drama in act III, scenes 1 and 2: a relationship where men and women can *mutually* be fully who they are in the drama of transforming love.

THE ONGOING STRUGGLE OF
TRANSFORMATION

The film ends with Lucia struggling with Tomas, shaking her head and running from his hold. A little girl dressed in a white veil and leading a tame goat has been apprehensively viewing the fight. She runs away laughing as she sees Lucia resist. We do not know if Lucia and Tomas will succeed in transforming their marriage but we do know that Lucia has never been more honest in telling Tomas that patriarchal marriage is unbearable. It is not too much to say that this little girl represents for Humberto Solas the next generation of Cuban women and the return of the archetype of the repressed feminine that will resist the wild passion of jealous and possessive sexuality.

In the beginning of the film, a battered woman shouts to the town: "Cubans, awaken!" But she is ignored and is harassed by Spanish troops. I believe that Solas was pointing out that this woman represents the lost personal, political/historical/sacred potential that women achieving their selfhood represent for Cuba. She symbolized the repressed feminine and the lives of women in the first two stages of Cuban history depicted in the film, 1895 and 1932, who demonstrate the potential strength of women. Yet they are unable to contribute and fully participate in a society because its body politic accepted as its official story the archetypal drama of patriarchy and the ways of life of emanation and deformation. The violence inherent in the sexism of patriarchy cripples both men and women. The tragedy is still with us. Castro in particular not only kept alive, but continues to reinforce, the archetypal drama of the male as conquering hero that reinforces the story of patriarchy.

The struggle is by no means over. This reminds us again of the appropriate use of the incomplete date, 196–. Thus for all Latinos the revolution in their depths and concrete lives is a continuous creation. Latina women are telling their own sacred stories that were silenced by the patriarchal drama. The web of emanation is now dying but the ways of life of incoherence and deformation as truncated failures and incomplete aspects of the core drama of transformation are choices that are available. Sadly, not enough

Latinos see the ending of the way of life of emanation as an opportunity to create a new wholeness in the way of life of transformation. Latina women are redefining who they are and, therefore, Latino men will be deeply affected. In some cases, this will mean divorce, separation, and much suffering.

But women are not blameless in the drama of patriarchy. Through covert manipulation, some Latinas continue to enjoy exercising power over their husbands and children. Moreover, women have had the prime duty for socializing the children and must take partial responsibility for perpetuating the dominance of the male over the female. This reality helps us to see how the sexism of the drama of patriarchy wounds both men and women. But all of this suffering will be meaningful only if it is redeemed by the creation of fundamentally new and better relationships between men and women.

Men, if they refuse to participate, will continue to wound and be wounded. Latino males must not lure women back into emanational relationships, nor continue to exercise illegitimate authority nor use violence to deform the family. Those Latino males who still live the story of patriarchy will have to empty themselves in act II, scene 2, of jealousy, of patriarchal culture, their repression of the feminine, a false sense of male honor and pride, and their lost security; and they must refuse to let go until the source of all sacred sources blesses them and renews them in act III. Perhaps like Alice Walker wrote, "God is an *it*," neither male nor female, neither white nor black, but the sacred is within us all.[17] It is necessary to wrestle like Jacob with the sacred until we *and* the sacred are transformed.

What was outstanding about Lucia was that she loved Tomas and *because* she loved him wanted to initiate a new and better relationship. Lucia was not rejecting him as a person but she was refusing to relate to him in the relationships of dependency, the archetypal drama of patriarchy, and the arrested ways of life of emanation and deformation that were destroying both of them. Lucia intuitively understood that she had to end this crippling story and the limited, inherited relationships of her marriage. For Lucia marriage is not the problem but a marriage in the service of emanation or deformation.

Because Tomas refused, Lucia had no choice but to resist and to love herself and Tomas enough to leave; because without this sacred core of authenticity she would have no self to give or to grow. Their old marriage was gone for good. But there are other choices.

In the way of life of transformation, Latinos have two faces: their own face and the face of God. As gods of transformation they can be creators themselves. What can they create? They can choose which of the eight archetypal relationships to use to deal with a problem, decide how long to nurture it, and when to break a connection in order to create a new coherence. For example, even subjection is redeemed in the way of life of transformation because Tomas could now refuse to allow Lucia to go to work on a particular day because she is not feeling well. In such a case Tomas would no longer be enacting the inherited, archetypal relationship of subjection to keep Lucia in the way of life of emanation, nor to use violence to destroy her new consciousness. In this case Tomas would be using subjection *temporarily* in order to protect Lucia so that she can eventually return to her job. Similarly all of the relationships can be re-created again and again to face new problems within the overarching way of life of transformation.

To truly love is to practice new archetypal dramas such as transforming love in the family. In this story each is an individual of unique importance and simultaneously the member of a thriving community because each is strengthened in their person. To love is to lead the other to their own sources within, to encourage new consciousness, relationships to others, creativity, and the struggle for shared goals in justice. Each is free to create conflict and change in order to continue to make common cause in the persistent shaping of the family. For young Latinos to see their mothers and fathers struggling to create new relationships, new archetypal dramas, and to participate with the god of transformation in shaping the world is to socialize, politicize, and make history for a whole new generation. To grow in such a lively environment is to see that each is sacred, men and women alike, that the world is shaped by people asking what they can and need to do together in the context of an open future that creates history so that human beings and the sacred can create an answer together.

Patriarchy is thus replaced by the archetypal drama of transforming love, which is a story within which each can practice the creation of relationships that fulfill in every way: fundamentally new and better linkages to self, to others, to the world, and to the sacred. The conquering hero who saved the damsel in distress is replaced by the vulnerable human person who acknowledges his or her need for the other in order to be human.

As in the movie *Lucia*, the verdict is never final.[18] Latino families need to continue to resist their inherited stories by redeeming their past. They will be condemned to repeat the past only if they remain ignorant of or refuse to heed the call that comes from within: each person is sacred and each has the right to live out their unique sacred journey. To struggle together as men and women in each other's destiny is to mutually assist one another in the creation of new archetypal dramas, the sacred stories of their lives.

But to resolve even our first problem through transformation requires us to become aware of all of the sources of our being that previously bound us, and helped to create this particular problem, and to reject these sources, even our previous way of life, and to look for help in the deepest depths. Though we have resolved only one problem, we now possess ineradicable theoretical knowledge: no concrete problem is concrete only or exists in isolation. It is always rooted in the archetypal cosmos. No problem can be resolved unless we journey to confront its roots in that cosmos: unless we learn how to uproot our connections even to the most embracing story of which any problem is a part, we shall not experience transformation. Every specific experience of transformation releases new energies earlier repressed and nourishes and enhances our capacity and desire to transform again. Every such experience, beginning with the first, enlarges our theoretical understanding of what we need to practice in every instance.[19]

MARRIED FOUR TIMES, TO THE SAME SPOUSE

Now that we are aware of the inherited stories of the Latino family and of the four ways of life, it is possible for us to know what we have been unconsciously living. But more important, we can now consciously and creatively *participate* in the core drama of transformation by choosing in which way of life to enact the stories of our lives. This allows us to get behind the label of family/ marriage and to determine the deeper and underlying meaning of our most important institution by asking the question: In the service of what way of life am I living family life? To this question there are four answers: either in the service of emanation, incoherence, deformation or transformation. Let us now see how in daily life an actual Latino family, that of Luis and Carmen whom we met in Chapter Three, rejected their inherited stories and chose to create different stories in the service of transformation.

Marriage in the Service of Emanation

When we last considered the family of Carmen and Luis we saw that they had inherited the story of patriarchy. They began their marriage and family in act I, scene 1 of the core drama arrested in the way of life of emanation. They were limited in their capacity to respond to problems by the relationships of dependency: emanation, subjection, isolation (psychological), buffering, and direct exchange. The story of patriarchy in the service of emanation dominated their personal, family life. As we have seen, in the public realm of their lives Carmen and Luis functioned very well as professional people who knew how to practice relationships not practiced at home: boundary management, incoherence, and isolation (physical) in the story of the market society in the service of incoherence in act II, scene 1 of the core drama.

Because of the autonomy experienced at work, Carmen became more aware of how untenable and unbearable her married life had become. Men on the job noticed Carmen's considerable beauty and skills and were attracted to her. This allowed Carmen's self-esteem to grow. She began exercising the relationships legitimized by the wider society in the public realm, especially the relationship of boundary management at home. This was a challenge to Luis and really an announcement that their previous marriage—based on keeping the wife dependent, loyal, and guilty in act I, scene 1 of the core drama in the story of patriarchy—was over. Carmen defied the relationships of emanation, subjection, isolation, buffering, and direct exchange at home. This meant that she had moved into act I, scene 2, wherein she was filled with a new inspiration, a new understanding of what marriage could be: two coequal persons with their own rights and duties. Carmen acted on this vision of marriage and broke her relationship with Luis by creating the relationship of incoherence: the two stood in the presence of each other and were afraid because they no longer knew how to relate nor how to remain married in a patriarchal family.

Marriage in the Service of Incoherence

Carmen and Luis were now in act II, scene 1 of the core drama. But rather than move on to act II, scene 2 and empty themselves of the story of patriarchy, they remained permanently at odds with each other and so turned the relationship of incoherence—that is, breaking with the story of patriarchy in the service of emanation— into the whole way of life of incoherence. But once again they were trapped. In the way of life of incoherence, persons turn their marriage and families into rational contracts. Carmen had her own car in her own name for the first time after twenty years of marriage; she spent money without accounting for it; dinner dates with colleagues, even males, became her right. Luis knew there was no way to go back and he did not want to. But he was threatened and confused by this new marriage.

What Carmen and Luis had brought about was not a transformation but a reformation. It was a reformation because the rebellion initiated by a new inspiration in act I, scene 2 stopped too soon by institutionalizing a permanent polarization into power positions in arresting the core drama in act II, scene 1, the whole way of life of incoherence. Both Carmen and Luis became a new kind of partial self, no longer loyal and guilty in an emanational relationship, but two powerful fragments as individuals pursuing their own separate lives in the market society and at home. This made their family life more efficient, organized, and well planned, but it also meant that much of the softening that was present due to the use of emanation and buffering as key relationships was now gone. Arguments took place over disputed rights and duties. The children, who were now older, were also given more independence but in return more was expected of them. The public realm of U.S. society and its official story, the way of life of incoherence, had effectively possessed their marriage and family.

But inherited stories do not go away simply by adopting another story in the truncated way of life of incoherence. Carmen and Luis had not successfully emptied themselves of the story of patriarchy; they took on a new story, the rational marriage that assimilated them into the way of life of incoherence in act II, scene 1. Carmen and Luis were rebelling against their past but stalled in the core drama they could not create anything better.

Archetypal dramas or the stories of our lives are sacred stories. If we are unaware of them, their power to possess us and drive us is unlimited. For this reason, the story of patriarchy and emanation as a way of life still remained as powerfully charged sacred fragments in the lives of Carmen and Luis. Flaunting autonomy and arguing at each other did not *exorcise* the lords of emanation present in the inherited patriarchal family. The stories of possessive love and patriarchy were enacted in the service of emanation. There was love, emotion, and passion present, although distorted. In the calculated power plays of the rational marriage and family, emotion, feelings, and affection are seen as weaknesses or ploys to return to the old ways. And yet unable to risk faith in their passions and emotions, Carmen and Luis became increasingly depressed. They both wanted to love in a way that freed them but they did not know how.

It was agreed in many conversations between them that they would not revert to the old emanational marriage and family. Yet they were stranded in a marriage that was at times comfortable but with no passion, love, surprises, or spontaneity. In order to escape this maddening impasse caught in two ways of life and two stories of marriage and family, Carmen made a decision to destroy her feelings for Luis and the children. She would now try to see them as distant relatives or cartoon figures in the distance. In this way she felt she would no longer be hurt by them nor would she cause pain in their lives. Now both she and Luis could pursue their own lives separately. But in making this "rational" decision, Carmen was actually reverting to the story of the battered woman in the service of emanation. Carmen was still caught up in fragments of the story of patriarchy. She blamed herself and wanted to remove herself as an obstacle from Luis's life so that he could be free. Carmen was willing once again to sacrifice her happiness. This was really for Carmen to think seriously of entering into deformation by consciously destroying her newly awakened self.

Marriage in the Service of Deformation

As a result of this kind of living, Carmen and Luis's sexual life became a desert. There was no passion and little pleasure. They were, after all, only fulfilling part of a contractual obligation. After a while the sex almost stopped completely. Luis was willing to go along with this death because he was afraid that if he had another affair Carmen would leave him for good. So to preserve a marriage and family founded on lingering fragments of the story of patriarchy and the story of rational power, Carmen and Luis stayed together. Luis, for his part, stated many times that their contract marriage had actually improved their standard of living so that the family was now economically "comfortable." But Luis's patriarchal face was also satisfied because as long as he collaborated with Carmen in killing their sexuality, she would always belong to him and to nobody else.

In this way the marriage deteriorated into becoming comfortably numb, a living death in the service of deformation; the marriage and family had become fundamentally worse. But our deepest sacred sources enter the story again and again. Luis broke the truce and had an affair. He was now prepared to end the marriage for everyone's sake. The cost was too high. Initially Carmen refused to deal with it. Then she wanted to end the marriage and family by getting out first. The family was in total incoherence. Carmen asked Luis to leave and he agreed. Now Carmen felt that for the first time she would be free. But what bewildered Carmen was that she still loved Luis. Was this merely a return to the way of life of emanation and the story of patriarchy with Luis taking her father's place? And what about Luis? Was this another patriarchal leftover allowing him to continue to hang onto Carmen as his personal possession? Perhaps. But there was also the possibility that if Luis and Carmen could *together* face their inherited stories and *together* empty themselves of the stories in act II, scene 2 then they could *together* enter into creating a fundamentally more loving marriage and family in act III, scenes 1 and 2.

The Fourth Marriage: Toward Transformation

Because of their inability, either alone or together, to confront their problems, Luis and Carmen realized the urgency of the situation and went into counseling. This was a very difficult step for both of them, because they came out of a tradition in which it was considered to be disloyal to talk about one's husband or wife to a stranger. In addition, to pay for therapy was unheard of for Latinos who come from a lower socioeconomic background. Such private matters that had to do with the honor and shame of the family were to be silently endured or mentioned only to one's most trusted relative, who usually advised patience and prayer.

What Carmen and Luis discovered in analysis was that they had been living inherited stories, the stories of others that denied and made impossible their capacity to create and live their own stories. Luis discovered aspects of his past that shocked him. He had been unconsciously living stories that made it unbearably painful for him to confront. He learned that he had been emotionally abandoned by his mother and so he developed a false independence that protected him from feeling too strongly the loss of love and affection. Due to this experience Luis was afraid of women and harbored an anger toward them that he had never recognized. Yet he craved love and affection. This story was projected onto Carmen when their first child was born. Carmen was no longer the lover; she had become *the* mother, identified with Luis's negative mother.

Carmen, for her part, realized that she was still afraid of her father. Although she was afraid of her father, she wanted to punish him and learned to control him by withdrawing from him. She thought her mother weak because she was controlled by her father. She recalled as a young girl often asking herself how it was possible for her to be so afraid of this man. As a result she wanted to relate to a man who would love her and free her from this constraint. Because of Luis's problems, he could not respond; Luis became too much like her father except that he was not as affected by her covert manipulation.

In addition, Luis discovered a deep wound that was due to the story of tribalism. As a youth Luis had been overwhelmed by sex. He attributed excessive sexual behavior to his Latino background. The wider society daily taught him to deny his heritage because it was made to appear ignorant and backward by the dominant society. His only escape would be to assimilate, to look and be like the powerful, to become white and acceptable and sexless. This conversion, or reformation, is what led to his determination to get his engineering degree. Many thought of Luis as a success, a role model, one of the so-called *better* Latinos because he was more like white people. But what was obscured by this apparent success was a very unhealthy split that took place in Luis's psyche. He split off the sexual, emotional, passionate face of his life from his intense, disciplined, clean, and hard-working face. Luis identified the sexually confusing side with the Latino heritage and so for a long time rejected the two together. He affirmed time and again his accepted, assimilated face as the competent and successful engineer, which he associated with the dominant society. Given this story, Luis was afraid of Carmen's passion as a Latina woman.

Through analysis Luis understood that he had to bring together the two faces of his being: the cognitive side with the underlying passion of life. What he needed to do was to empty himself not only of the devastating story of patriarchy but also of the story of racism/tribalism that led him to want to assimilate and in so doing hate himself and his own heritage. In this way he needed to reacquire his sexuality and passion and reintegrate it as part of his story as a Latino male. What both Carmen and Luis learned from their counseling sessions during a period of two years was that both of them also had a great deal of work to do separately because each had brought to the marriage their own personal problems that were exacerbated by each other.

CONCLUSION

When I last spoke to Carmen and Luis, they were struggling to successfully enter into act II, scene 2 of the core drama of transformation. They sought on the deeper level to empty themselves of the inherited Latino and assimilated Anglo marriages and family life that they had lived in the service of the ways of life of emanation, incoherence, and deformation. For the past two years they have been talking, analyzing, and fighting together and individually to avoid slipping back into the inherited Latino stories and the official story of power and assimilation of U.S. society. Let us recall that in act II, scene 1 we break with the persons with whom we were previously linked in emanation in act I, and we refuse to remain partial and stunted. This rupture with the past enacts the relationship of incoherence: we stand in the presence of others and refuse to relate in a way that cripples everybody.

What Luis and Carmen had done was to take the relationship of incoherence as a breaking experience and turn it into the whole way of life of incoherence wherein they both pursued self-interest and power in a rational family and marriage. But now both of them *together* have entered into incoherence with this way of life and have also rejected the destructive death of deformation. But to break and reject is only part of the process. They have to wait for a new spirit, a new story to take root in them. Until this happens they cannot enter successfully into act III, scenes 1 and 2.

There is no doubt that Carmen and Luis's family and marriage are better. The limited repertory of relationships of the inherited Latino past that kept Latina women in dependence has been successfully rejected. The wounding story of patriarchy is in full retreat. The deadly assimilation of the family into contractual relationships in the service of incoherence is now unbearable. Luis and Carmen are always on their guard against the story of the battered woman and the tendency of the Latino male's search for the eternal mother in their wives. Both are now free to enact the story of transforming love and to use all eight relationships in the service of transformation. Carmen travels and is fully supported by Luis in her efforts to have time alone. The two protect each other, care deeply for one another, and do whatever is necessary to help the other in her or his job. They also have the right to say no to each other and to disagree. The lives of the children still living at home has also improved dramatically. There is no longer constant strain and hostility in the house. For the first time open affection and tenderness take place between husband and wife. The family meets together to discuss matters of concern to individuals and to all.

Nevertheless Carmen and Luis are fully aware that there is still much to be done. Neither has fully succeeded in getting rid of the stories with which they came into the marriage. It is a constant struggle to make sure that the stories of patriarchy, the negative mother, possessive love, the battered woman, and power do not overwhelm them again. Both must take care that they do not lull each other into a false collusion where they keep each other satisfied but unfulfilled. There needs to be an openness and willingness to risk the relationship of emanation time and again, but this time in the service of transformation. All new inspirations and creative moments of love begin as overwhelming experiences of emanation in act I, scene 2. What turned eruptions of the fundamentally new into frozen moments of truth is that the experience did not lead to development and growth and become a transforming experience.

However, in the service of transformation, emanation is now free to come forth in the form of new ideas, loving relationships, and events. In this way the source of all deepest sources continues to speak in our lives.

I had hoped in this final chapter to tell a more successful and pleasing story that ended with transformation in act III, scenes 1 and 2. I am sure that in some aspects of their lives, Carmen and Luis have experienced transformation, but in regard to their marriage and family they have not, as yet. There is no doubt, based on the understanding gained from extensive interviewing, that Luis and Carmen are enacting relationships daily *toward* transformation without having actually brought about a new marriage and family. But this is where most of us are. We are asking new questions and breaking new ground. Like Lucia and Tomas, Carmen and Luis are struggling to maintain integrity and to keep their marriage and family authentic. Luis and Carmen have agreed to talk, to be honest, not to revert to the power plays and guilt of the past stories. The marriages and family in the service of emanation, incoherence, and deformation are over. Now what remains is to create their own marriage and family, a marriage and family of mutual love and vulnerability in the service of transformation.

In my final interviews with Luis and Carmen, they were hopeful but unsure if their attempt to create a new marriage and family in the service of transformation would be accomplished. What they did know was that never before had they realized as clearly the demands upon them. They know it will not be easy and they will have to go all the way to make it work. Occasionally they relapse into long periods of avoidance and silence while the business of life goes on. But underlying all of the noise of everyday life is the constant urging that comes from within: they may at times get tired of the struggles of transformation but transformation is not tired of them.

NOTES

1. See Manfred Halpern's analysis of the archetypal drama of democracy in "Choosing Between Ways of Life and Death and Between Forms of Democracy: An Archetypal Analysis," *Alternatives*, January 1987, pp. 5–34.

2. For a further explanation of the sacred in the lives of Latinos, see Chapters Five and Six in David T. Abalos, *Latinos in the United States: The Sacred and the Political* (Notre Dame, Ind.: University of Notre Dame Press, 1986).

3. Manfred Halpern, "The Political Faces of All Archetypes," a paper given at a conference at Hofstra University on C. G. Jung and the Humanities.

4. Manfred Halpern, "Transformation: Its Theory and Practice in Personal, Political, Historical and Sacred Being," Unpublished manuscript.

5. For an excellent analysis of patriarchy, see Gerda Lerner, *The Creation of Patriarchy* (New York: Oxford University Press, 1986).

6. Abalos, *Latinos in the United States*, Chapter Three, "The Politics of the Latino Family."

7. See Takeo Doi, *The Anatomy of Dependence*, trans. John Bester (Tokyo: Kodansha International, 1973). Doi is a Japanese psychiatrist who documents the debilitating need for dependency by exploring the role of *amae*, which parallels our use of the relationship of emanation. This book confirms the cross-cultural ability of our theory to point out universal and necessary ways of relating.

8. For a good study of the alchemists as transformers, see Titus Burckhardt, *Alchemy* (Baltimore: Penguin, 1971).

9. For a first-rate analysis of liberal individualism, see Marshall Berman, *The Politics of Authenticity* (New York: Atheneum, 1972), especially, pp. 113–159.

10. Halpern, "Transformation," Chapter 4, Part II, is one of the best and most penetrating analyses that I have read regarding the utter bankruptcy of living in the service of incoherence within liberal society, which is really settling for "organized insecurity" because we do not know how or are unwilling to transform the incoherence.

11. Ibid., p. 119.

12. For a frightening example of the way of life of deformation practiced by Latinos, see Robert Lindsley, "Worlds in Collision: From Barrio to Harvard to Jail," *New York Times*, July 26, 1987. This article tells the story of Jose Razo who, in order to escape the incoherence of living between two worlds—the Latino characterized by poverty and values of *familia* and the Anglo world of power characterized by privilege and status—created a new and worse world. He joined the Cholos, a term used by second-generation Chicanos to describe a whole life-style and indeed a tribal existence. Jose turned to this group to give him an identity, a code of honor and behavior that included armed robbery.

13. There are many other Latino novels, short stories, and films that can be fruitfully analyzed through the perspective of our theory of transformation. For example, *La Carreta* by the Puerto Rican essayist and

playwright Rene Marques (Rio Piedras, P.R.: Editorial Cultural, 1971); *Woman Hollering Creek*, by Sandra Cisneros (New York: Random House, 1991); *The Salt of the Earth*, a 1952 film by Harry Biberman regarding Chicanos in the United States; and Alice Walker's *The Color Purple* (New York: Washington Square Press, 1982), the novel that has taught me so much about male/female relationships in the African-American community and in other communities of color surrounded by networks of racism, classism, and sexism.

14. See Gregory J. Massell, "Law as an Instrument of Revolutionary Change in a Traditional Milieu: The Case of Soviet Central Asia," *Law and Society Review*, 2, no. 2 (February 1968), for a similar intervention to break patterns of male authority.

15. The Nation of Islam faced a similar threat with drug addicts. Malcolm X described the six stages by which black people freed themselves from dependence on drugs. Part of the therapy was to transfer the need for dope to one's need for community. But unless a further step was taken— that is, to lead a person back to her or his own sacredness so that they are free to choose—it was possible to simply transfer the loyalty from a substance to the newfound narcotic of an overwhelming mystery in charismatic leaders and/or a group. See Malcolm X, *The Autobiography of Malcolm X*, with the assistance of Alex Haley (New York: Grove Press, 1966), pp. 260–262.

16. Berman (in *The Politics of Authenticity*) uses this phrase in his analysis of Rousseau's protagonist, Julie, in *La Nouvelle Eloise* as she rejects her authenticity (pp. 241–257).

17. As an example of the struggle of Celie as an African-American woman to assert her personal sacredness over and against the story of patriarchy, see Alice Walker's *The Color Purple*, pp. 175–179.

18. For an intelligent and thorough review of *Lucia*, see Anne-Marie Taylor's analysis in *The Film Quarterly*, 28, no. 2 (April 1974), pp. 53–59.

19. Halpern, "Transformation," Chapter 4.

Bibliography

Abalos, David T. *Latinos in the United States: The Sacred and the Political* (Notre Dame, Ind.: University of Notre Dame Press, 1986).

Abalos, David T. "Rediscovering the Sacred Among Latinos: A Critique from the Perspective of a Theory of Transformation." *The Latinos Studies Journal*, 3, no. 2, (May 1992).

Abalos, David T. "The Teacher as Guide." *Journal of Dharma*, 11, no. 1 (January-March 1986).

Abalos, David T. "Transformative Commitment: A New Paradigm for the Study of the Religious." *Journal of Dharma*, 6, no. 3 (July-September 1981).

Berman, Marshall. *The Politics of Authenticity* (New York: Atheneum, 1972).

Biberman, Harry, director, *Salt of the Earth*, 1952.

Blea, Irene I. *La Chicana and the Intersection of Race, Class, and Gender* (New York: Praeger, 1992).

Brown, L. Carl and Norman Itzkowitz, eds. "Four Contrasting Repertories of Human Relations in Islam: Two Pre-Modern and Two Modern Ways of Dealing with Continuity and Change, Collaboration and Conflict and Achieving Justice," *Psychological Dimensions of Near Eastern Studies* (Princeton, N.J.: The Darwin Press, 1977).

Burckhardt, Titus. *Alchemy* (Baltimore: Penguin, 1971).

Cisneros, Sandra. *Woman Hollering Creek* (New York: Random House, 1991).

Doi, Takeo. *The Anatomy of Dependence*. Trans. John Bester (Tokyo: Kodansha International, 1973).

Duany, Luis and Karen Pittman. *Latino Youths at a Crossroads.* An Adolescent Pregnancy Prevention Clearinghouse report by the Children's Defense Fund, January-March 1990. (CDF Publications, 122 C Street N.W., Washington, D.C. 20001.)

"For Children: A Fair Chance, Stop Wasting Lives and Money." *New York Times,* September 6, 1987, editorial page.

Gephart, Martha A. and Robert Pearson. "Contemporary Research on the Urban Underclass." *Items,* 42, no. 12 (June 1988). (A publication of the Social Science Research Council, 605 Third Avenue, New York, NY 10158.)

Halberstam, David. *The Best and the Brightest* (New York: Random House, 1972).

Halpern, Manfred. "Choosing Between Ways of Life and Death Between Forms of Democracy: An Archetypal Analysis." *Alternatives: A Journal of World Politics,* Winter 1986–87. (Published by the Center for the Study of Developing Societies, Delhi, India, and the Institute for World Order, New York.)

Halpern, Manfred. "Four Contrasting Repertories of Human Relations in Islam: Two Pre-Modern and Two Modern Ways of Dealing with Continuity and Change, Collaboration and Conflict and Achieving Justice. In *Psychological Dimensions of Near Eastern Studies,* L. Carl Brown and Norman Itzkowitz, eds. (Princeton, N.J.: The Darwin Press, 1977).

Halpern, Manfred. "Notes on the Theory and Practice of Transformation." Unpublished manuscript, Princeton University, 1980.

Halpern, Manfred. "The Political Faces of All Archetypes." A paper given at a conference of Hofstra University on C. G. Jung and the Humanities.

Halpern, Manfred. "Transformation: Its Theory and Practice in Personal, Political, Historical and Sacred Being." Unpublished manuscript.

Halpern, Manfred. "Why Are Most of Us Partial Selves? Why Do Partial Selves Enter the Road into Deformation?" A paper delivered at the 1991 Annual Meeting of the American Political Science Association, Washington, D.C.

Institute for Puerto Rican Policy. "Data on the Puerto Rican Community." No. 4 (March 1986).

Kayal, Philip M. *Bearing Witness: Gay Man's Health Crisis and the Politics of AIDS* (San Francisco: Westview Press, 1993).

Lerner, Gerda. *The Creation of Patriarchy* (New York: Oxford University Press, 1986).

Lewis, Oscar. *Five Families* (New York: New American Library, 1959).

Lindsley, Robert. "Worlds in Collision: From Barrio to Harvard to Jail." *New York Times,* July 26, 1987.

Mahfouz, Naguib. *Palace Walk* (New York: Doubleday, 1990).

Malcolm X. *The Autobiography of Malcolm X*, with the assistance of Alex Haley (New York: Grove Press, 1966).

Marques, Rene. *La Carreta* (Rio Piedras, P.R.: Editorial Cultural, 1971).

Massell, Gregory J. "Law as an Instrument of Revolutionary Change in a Traditional Milieu: The Case of Soviet Central Asia." *Law and Society Review*, 2, no. 2 (February 1968).

McIntyre, Robert S. "The Populist Tax Act of 1989." *The Nation*, April 2, 1988.

Nasar, Sylvia. "The 1980's: A Very Good Time for the Very Rich." *New York Times*, March 2, 1992.

New York Times, December 1, 1991.

Pagels, Elaine. *The Gnostic Gospels* (New York: Random House, 1979).

Paz, Octavio. "The Sons of La Malinche." In *Introduction to Chicano Studies: A Reader*, Livia Isauro Duran and H. Russell Bernard, eds. (New York: Macmillan, 1973).

Paz, Octavio. *Sor Juana*, Margaret Sayers Peden, trans. (Cambridge, Mass.: Harvard University Press, 1988).

Perez, Maria E. *Lo Americano en el Teatro de Sor Juana Ines de la Cruz* (New York: Eliseo Torres and Sons, 1975).

Piven, Frances Fox and Richard A. Cloward. *The New Class War* (New York: Pantheon Books, 1982).

Report to President Bowen on the Status of Latinos at Princeton University. Princeton University, May 2, 1985.

Riding, Alan. *Distant Neighbors: A Portrait of the Mexicans* (New York: Alfred A. Knopf, 1985).

Robb, Stewart. *Parsifal Libretto*, English version (New York: G. Schirmer, n.d.).

Sharabi, Hisham. *Neopatriarchy: A Theory of Distorted Change in Arab Society* (New York: Oxford University Press, 1988).

Shockley, John. *Chicano Revolt in a Texas Town* (Notre Dame, Ind.: University of Notre Dame Press, 1974).

The Status of Puerto Ricans in the United States. Published by The National Congress for Puerto Rican Rights, Centro de Estudios Puerto-riquenos, Hunter College, City University of New York, May 1987.

Taylor, Anne-Marie. *The Film Quarterly*, 28, no. 2 (April 1974).

Ulanov, Ann Belford. *The Feminine* (Evanston, Ill.: Northwestern University Press, 1972).

Walker, Alice. *The Color Purple* (New York: Washington Square Press, 1982).

Young, Iris M. *Justice and the Politics of Difference* (Princeton, N.J.: Princeton University Press, 1990).

Index

Abalos, David T., 43, 61
al-Farabi, 8
Anglo-Saxon cultural traits, xxi, 58
Archetypal, 2–5, 9–14, 51; analysis, xv, xxii–xxiii, 13, 82, 111, 119; description of eight relationships, 18–35, dramas, xv–xxii, 2–4, 9–11, 17–19, 24–29, 33–34, 40–41, 63–71, 81, 88, 91, 116–118, 124–133; enact eight relationships, 116, 119, 123; journey, 4, 6–9, 38, 120; process of breaking and recreating, 115–116, 120, 124–125, 140; process of transformation rejects the fixed lords of orthodoxy, 5; repeat same dramas, 134; underlying forming transpersonal sources, 106, 116, 141; ways of life, definition of, xvii, 14–17, 25, 48–49, 60, 116–119, 132
Archetype, 8, 10–13, 75; creating

new archetypes, xv, 124, 133, 140; definition of, xvi, 8, 116; incarnating of, sacred sources, 1, 3–5, 10, 13–14, 31, 36–38, 116–117; two faces, 6
Arabi, Ibn, 8
Aristotle, 46
assimilation, 31, 69; acceptance of way of life of incoherence, 54–56; as self-hatred, 54–56; cost of, 54–56, 123; role of Catholic Church in, 25; role of religion in, 25, 55; significance of for Latinos, 54–56, 79, 84, 123, 147–148
authority, xiii, xv, 20–26, 32–35, 46, 50–55, 57, 74, 118; breakdown of for Latino parents, 107–108, 126; patriarchal, 126, 129, 135, 139
Aztecs, 52, 88

biculturalism/bilingualism, 78
Blake, William, 8

Boehme, Jacob, 8
Boff, Leonardo, 8
Bonino, Miguel, 8
boundary management, 16, 26–
   27; definition and description
   of, 26, 131–132; family and use
   of in the service of incoherence,
   26–28, 123, 142, 144; forbidden relationship for Latinos,
   119, 131–134; institutionalized
   power, 26, 132; new way of relating for Latinos, 26–27, 142;
   poverty due to lack of, 27; re-
   created in the service of transformation, 26, 132; structural
   violence and, 26; U.S. society
   and, 26–27
Bruno, Giordano, 8
Buddha, 8
buffering, 16, 20, 28–30, 33, 50;
   antirevolutionary use in the
   family and society, 22, 29, 32,
   90, 129–130, 132, 143; definition and description, 20, 129–
   130; re-created and enacted in
   the service of transformation,
   132; relationship of dependence
   for Latina women, 22, 119, 142
Bush, George, xiii, 47

Carmen: arrested in act I, scene 1,
   70, 142; as partial self, 143;
   creating new archetypal relationships and stories, 142, 148;
   marriage in the service of emanation, 70–74, 142; patriarchy
   and, 70–77, 142–145, 148; rebelling against the inherited Latino story of the family, 74,
   142–144, 146; reformation not
   transformation, 143; story of
   Luis and, xxii, 68, 70–77, 142–

149. See also Luis; Luis's family
   and marriage
Catholic Church: assimilating
   force for Latinos, 25, 52–53;
   Charismatic movement among
   Latinos, 19; Latin America and,
   8, 25; Latinos and, 25, 52–53;
   liberation theology and, 8
Chavez, Cesar, 27
concreteness: enacting new forms
   of eight relationships, 17, 34;
   giving direction to the undifferentiated, 6, 13; inherited manifestations of, 14
continual creation: human participation in, 23–24
core drama of transformation,
   xxii, 1–6, 11–19, 23, 48–61,
   70, 82–84, 97, 110–111, 120–
   126; acts and scenes, 120–126,
   129, 135; as archetypal drama,
   evident in, 111; as sacred journey, 117; continuous creation
   and, 24, 111–112, 117; definition and description, 120–126;
   exiting from, 51, 97, 136; trav-
   eling through, 38, 48–50; turning point, 121, 136, 147
countertradition, 8

deformation: definition and description, xvi, 5, 11–12, 56–57,
   93, 123, 134; exit from the core
   drama of transformation, 4, 35,
   38–39, 97, 104, 136; fragility of
   as a way of life, 37, 72, 88; increasingly replaces emanation
   and incoherence, 5, 25, 40, 91,
   123–124, 136; Latino marriage
   and family and, 144–145; lord
   of nothing and, 12, 117; most

About the Author

DAVID T. ABALOS is Professor of Religious Studies and Sociology at Seton Hall University. He has lectured and written extensively on multicultural and gender scholarship and on Latinos in the United States from the perspective of the politics of transformation. He is the author of *Chicanos in the United States: Redeeming the Past, Transforming the Future* and *Latinos in the United States: The Sacred and the Political.*